A Jewish Girl & a Not-So-Jewish Boy

A Memoir from New Jersey to Hawaii

By Sandra M. Z. Armstrong

Text copyright © 2014 Sandra M. Z. Armstrong
All Rights Reserved
ISBN: 0692244670
ISBN 13: 9780692244678
Library of Congress Control Number: 2014911710

Sandra M.Z. Armstrong, Kailua, HI

Dedications

To Deborah Heart and Lung Center in Browns Mills, New Jersey, and its founder, Dora Moness Shapiro, who believed:

"There is no price on life."

To Temple Israel in Ridgewood, New Jersey, where our journey began

To Congregation Sof Ma'arav in Honolulu, Hawaii, where our journey continues

To Aunt Rose and Uncle Bernie who were my parents when my own parents couldn't be

To my children, remember to live your lives like an open book. Each day is a clean page to fill with acts of loving-kindness.

To my husband, Donald, who promised me "a wild and crazy ride."

Prologue

At a family holiday dinner, do you secretly hide the pork, ham, or bacon under the table? *A Jewish Girl & a Not-So-Jewish Boy* addresses this and other awkward situations.

It is my hope that people of interfaith marriages will begin to tell their own stories. The children of these couples will learn what each parent believes and why. These accounts will be "spiritual histories" of their religious values. Just as our forefathers passed on their oral traditions, today we can create our own interfaith oral traditions. By doing so, parents and grandparents will fortify future generations with their inspirational memories.

Donald converted to Judaism after twenty-five years of marriage. We moved to Hawaii shortly after his conversion for an extended honeymoon. As we quickly discovered, people who live in Hawaii spend time listening to each other and "talking story." The spirit of aloha is like the Jewish tradition of welcoming the stranger. Just as Abraham opened his tent for strangers and kindly welcomed them, so do the people of Hawaii. We are grateful to live in a place where our differences and traditions are celebrated.

Reflections inspired by my walks along the soft, sandy beaches of Hawaii are included at the end of our story. Each reflection correlates to a chapter in my life.

Acknowledgements

To Sof Ma'arav Book Club, for the book's *first* reading and critical review. To Rabbi Morris Goldfarb, of blessed memory, whose suggestions I followed. To all our friends at Congregation Sof Ma'arav who guided me including Francine Margulies, Naomi Olstein, Robert Littman, and Deborah Washofsky for reviewing the manuscript. To Gin and Mat Sgan for their continual support of this project. To my in-laws, Janet and James Armstrong, for their love and understanding. To my sister Bobbie, and cousins Amy, Lois, and Martin. To Don's brother Jesse, our sister-in-law Debbie, and our niece Katie. To Uncle Alan, of blessed memory, who called me after reading the manuscript to say, "Your mother's illness was not your fault." To our second-generation cousins, Michelle, Michael, Stacy, Emily, Laura, Richie, Rachel, and David for the lively memories of Hanukkah parties and Passover Seders. To our wonderful friends in New Jersey who inspired us to go for our dreams. To Leon Cilliers and Sheila Blecher Kuniyoshi for their assistance. To Rabbi Kerry Olitzky for supporting outreach to interfaith families. To Rabbi Noam Marans and Rabbi Amy Roth, and Rabbi Gil Steinlauf and Rabbi Batya Steinlauf for their spiritual guidance. To Gertrude Bonatti-Zotta, of blessed memory, for her passionate years of volunteer service at Deborah Hospital. And finally, to my ninety-four-year-old mentor, Mrs. Louis Hamilton, who told me to finish the book.

Table of Contents

Prologue ...v

Acknowledgements ...vii

One: We Met ...1

Two: I Didn't Die ...11

Three: I Can't Read Hebrew ...19

Four: A Day to Rest ...25

Five: Kindness to Strangers ...31

Six: Jumping Into Judaism ...35

Seven: Growing Up ...46

Eight: Let's Move to Hawaii ...62

Nine: A Conversion ...69

Ten: The Mikvah ...73

Eleven: Under the Huppah ...77

Epilogue ...87

Bibliography ...93

Reflections Along Hawaiian Shores ...95

One: We Met

My husband Donald was raised without guilt. I found this amazing. I often questioned him about family matters: "Don't you feel guilty about that?" His response was, "It is what it is. I'm neither the cause nor the blame." How refreshing. Perhaps I was attracted to him because of his "no guilt factor." Don admitted when he was wrong and made amends as necessary. He was not weighed down with guilt like I was.

I met Donald at Rutgers College in New Jersey. He was a year ahead of me in the class of 1975 (the last all-male class) and I was in the first class of women, the class of 1976. Don was notorious for hanging around the girl's dormitory playing his guitar while sitting on the floor out in the hallway. He kept a toothbrush in his back pocket because he never knew what might turn up. I thought he was witty and handsome, but somehow I thought he would be better off without me. I was "into dating" other men and he seemed like a sensitive guy who might get hurt easily. My instincts told me to stay away because I did not want to become seriously involved at the time. Plus my roommate, Melissa, liked him and so did Becky, our friend down the hall—not a good situation in which to pursue a guitar-playing collegian.

By my junior year, I no longer lived with Melissa and I was a free agent. One afternoon, as I walked down College Avenue with my friend Sari, Donald stepped off the Rutgers shuttle bus wearing an aloha shirt, khakis, and slippers (known as flip-flops on the mainland). I thought he was funny but weird. Without hesitating, he asked me out for Saturday night. Caught off guard, I answered yes. When he left, I immediately turned to Sari and announced, "I can't believe I just said yes." In my mind I heard the warnings of Melissa who was still really mad at him for something or other.

On our first date, we attended a play at the local college theater and thoroughly enjoyed ourselves. In fact, I liked him a lot. The next weekend, we hopped on a train for a date in New York City. Don was wearing what I considered a pink suit. He said it was actually a red weave, but it looked pink to me. We dined near Madison Square Garden at a wonderful Italian restaurant. He was hoping that I wouldn't finish my veal, so he could eat the rest. I complained about how stuffed I was, but to his disappointment, I finished every last bite. As a college wrestler, Don was well built and functioned on an extremely high metabolism. He often polished off several meals at one sitting. This fancy restaurant did not offer a menu, so we had no idea how much the meal was going to cost (a potential embarrassment for any young man out to impress his date). Anyway, it wasn't too expensive and the evening was a huge success. I was smitten. As we walked along Mine Street in New Brunswick on the way back to my rooming house, Don pulled leaves off trees and ate them. I thought how strange. But he impressed me with his knowledge of edible foliage.

We dated regularly. He attempted to help me conquer Economics 101, but I had to struggle nightly to get a "C." Tearfully, I admitted that it made no sense to me, and I wondered how he could be so smart. He didn't really help me, anyway. He just wanted to hang around while I studied.

He was not "into" my theater crowd either, although I was very serious about my acting courses. At one cast party, he sat on the stoop outside of the rooming house positioned as a gargoyle statue. He was poking fun at all of us (and himself), being irritating and attractive all at once. I didn't know where this relationship was going, but I did know that I was thrilled to be with him. The deciding factor (over other boyfriends) was that he stood up straight and often reminded me to stand up straight too. Raised by parents in the military, he learned the importance of correct posture. He was no slouch. Don was everything I wanted in a guy, handsome, funny, and smart. I knew he would make a good husband, provider, and father. Yes, he was quirky, but so was I.

He was brave, too. When I moved out of the dorms into an apartment on Mine Street during my senior year, he showed great promise as my future protector. For the first time in my college experience, I had a single room. Don't get too excited because my bedroom was the size of a pantry off the kitchen. Actually, it was the pantry. I had enough room for a dresser, mattress, door, and window. It was paradise.

Before moving in, we tackled a collective apartment clean up. The kitchen was a good a place to start, and probably the most in need of our immediate attention. Don said, "Let's look under this bench over here." He yanked it from the wall spilling thousands of roaches all over the kitchen floor. The sight of the bug-infested bench lifted high in the air caused all my roommates, including me, to run around the kitchen screaming. Like Superman, Don kept his cool, lifted the bench, and tossed it outside. This is a man who knew his bugs because he was an accomplished Eagle Scout. I was so impressed with this daring act that I decided he was the one for me.

While Don was staying over in my apartment, one of my college roommates called to him in the middle of the night. Jodi was in her babydoll pajamas standing in the bathroom yelling. "There's a man peeking through the window at me." Barely awake, Don was sure that it was her imagination. But Jodi kept insisting that there was a prowler. Don slowly got out of bed, walked into the bathroom, and found a man staring back at him through the window. Okay, so much for certainty. Don bravely stood his ground and the man ran away. Again, I thought I would love to have a man like this around my house.

Don and I got along extremely well, except when we fought and broke up. When I was a senior at Rutgers, he was a graduate student in the business school at New York University. He lived with his grandparents in Leonia, New Jersey, and commuted to school in New York City. On weekends, he came to see me in New Brunswick. He would arrive on Friday, we would have a super weekend together and then we would break up. He would leave, and I would cry. This was not your usual courtship by any means. One time, we broke up within the first few hours of his arrival, and he hopped back on the next bus home. This courtship made my heart ache. We were certain that every time we broke up, it was for the best, and we promised to remain friends.

We reconciled during the week with endless phone conversations. Don's grandfather continually complained about the phone usage. He yelled, "How could you possibly have so much to say to each other?" Good question. Now that we have been married for over thirty-seven years, I wonder about that too.

Neither of us wanted to make the big commitment, and we were afraid because our religions were different. Don was raised Presbyterian and I was born Jewish. This represented a significant challenge to us. My childhood consisted of a limited religious background. My parents did not join the Conservative synagogue in Highland Park, New Jersey. All my friends went to Hebrew school and celebrated Bar/Bat Mitzvahs (coming of age for a Jewish adult), but I did not. Nonetheless, I knew I was Jewish and my family celebrated the holidays of Passover and Hanukkah. On the High Holidays, Rosh Hashanah and Yom Kippur, I went to the synagogue with my friends. We huddled outside the sanctuary and occasionally eavesdropped on the service. That was the extent of my Jewish education, and yet, I understood that I was and would remain a Jew.

Don was raised on military bases and introduced to chaplains of many faiths. He had a universal base for his religious observance, but he was raised as a Presbyterian in a Christian home. His grandmother, Louise, read gospel everyday and quoted the Bible often. She found great peace in her spirituality. Don's belief in God was solid.

We didn't see how this was going to work. Our dissimilar backgrounds were troublesome. Still, I was heartbroken every time we split up at the end of the weekend before his return to Leonia on Sunday nights. I missed him so much, and I would cry and cry over what I thought was the end of our relationship. I eventually mustered the strength to stop this heart-wrenching pattern. I decided to not talk to him for a full week. This was hard because he kept calling and calling the apartment to make amends, but I instructed my roommates to tell him that I wasn't available. I remember Jodi reporting back to me on his sorry state. Something had to change, so I had to use what I thought to be an extreme measure.

It worked. Not long after the week of separation through phone postponement, we decided to get engaged! What a relief. But one issue had to be addressed: the religion of our future children. I told him that I knew the children would be considered Jewish coming from a Jewish mother, but I also wanted my children to be raised in my faith, attend synagogue, and have a Bar/Bat Mitzvah. Did he see any problems with this? Could he reconcile this? He said he understood my feelings and agreed. Raising our children, as Jews, would be fine. I needed to hear this.

Don proposed in March 1977 at a Hawaiian-themed restaurant in New York City called the Hawaii Kai. It featured a large, cardboard, lava-spewing volcano. Lights twinkled among fake jungle fauna and plastic Plumeria blossoms. The tackiness of the décor could not detract from the splendor of the evening. Over "swimming pool" blue drinks topped with tiny parasols and pineapples, Don gave me his great-grandmother's white-gold engagement ring. The ring was a size eight and I wore a size four, so I kept it on my thumb throughout the dinner and all through the night. For some unknown reason, the diamonds in the center of the ring formed a Jewish star. I considered this a good sign for our future. I was thrilled to be marrying Donald! No more break ups and no more Sunday night separations that tore me up.

We decided to get married in October. However, when Don finished his MBA course work in June and began working in the city, his grandparents told him that it was time for him to move out on his own. Well, not without me! During a busy Fourth of July weekend, we excitedly planned to get married in two weeks. We phoned everyone to announce our upcoming wedding because we didn't have time for invitations. This was different, but fast and efficient. We shopped for our wedding attire during a delightful trip with my parents to the Woodbridge Mall. I bought a fashionable short, white, stretchy polyester dress. Don bought a new suit and a blue, pointy-collared silk shirt decorated with miniature sailboats—courtesy of my Dad. We thought we were so cool, a combination of seventies and disco.

The Mayor of Highland Park, Mayor Berman, married us in his office with our immediate family present. I couldn't believe how nervous I was on my wedding day. Yet, I was certain of something: I saw myself happy for the rest of my life with this man. Both of us were only twenty-three years old. What did we know? I knew in my heart that we would be good together. Mayor Berman offered Don three options for the wedding: a short one, a medium one, or a Jewish-style one, with the breaking of a wine glass at the end of the ceremony—we provided the glass. It was unexpected and nice to have so many options. Our vows were taken and we were married after the broken glass splintered under Don's shoe. The shattering of the glass represented the fragileness of the Jewish people, and even though we were at the height of celebration, we needed to remember the past. Afterward, we joined college friends and the rest of the family at my parents' house for a backyard garden party. It was strange and amazing to be husband and wife. My Dad had us pose multiple times that evening in our wedding attire, but unfortunately he forgot to remove the lens cap on the camera.

We honeymooned at the Jersey Shore in Cape May for a long weekend. As Don displayed his expertise on the surfboard, I had a glimpse of the life he had led as a teenager on army bases in

Hawaii. Don went to middle school at Central Intermediate and then to Leilehua High. He played football, wrestled, and surfed. Don loved those years in Hawaii before his family relocated to Virginia. We began our new lives together while he reminisced about this special time. As we strolled around quaint streets of historic Cape May nibbling on popcorn and fudge, we leisurely contemplated the endless possibilities of our future.

Our first place together was an apartment in Leonia, New Jersey. We had an easy commute by bus to our jobs in New York City. Don's work was in investment banking and I worked in magazine publishing. We couldn't decide who should do the house work, so neither of us did any. We spent all day Saturday washing dishes and cleaning up. Sometimes the dishes got so piled up in the sink that we put them in the bathtub and turned on the shower. We felt this was an efficient cleaning method.

I didn't know how to cook. On our first day of our domestic life, I boiled water for coffee and burned the teapot. Don knew he was in trouble. He said, "Your Mom is such a good cook, what happened?" I suppose I married him under a false assumption of a lifetime of homemade meals. But the good news is that Don had worked at a Sizzler steak house during high school and had become familiar with cuts of beef. During a food-shopping excursion one afternoon, he gave me a tour of the meat case. When we got home, Don demonstrated how to clean and cook a chicken. I was so grossed out that I vowed never to eat chicken again.

Every week we loaded up our "Aunt Mary" shopping cart. I dubbed it "Aunt Mary" because my beloved aunt walked the streets of my hometown with one just like it. For some reason, Don insisted on buying cans of tomato paste. He said you could never have enough tomato paste. I didn't understand why, but I didn't argue with him. Every week we pushed our Aunt Mary shopping cart and walked a mile to the center of downtown Leonia. We hooked our dry cleaning over the cart full of groceries, including all the tomato paste and other assorted canned goods that Don was so fond of. If we weren't careful and didn't balance it just right, our cart would fall over in the middle of the street. This occurred at least once during every shopping spree, spilling a variety of essential canned goods into the street.

We didn't have a car our first year of married life because we commuted by bus into the city. Walking to retrieve all our possible necessities over the weekend suited us fine until, after a year of blissful, no-car-hassle living, Uncle Bernie offered to sell us his pink station wagon for a dollar. It efficiently got us around town except for one picture perfect Sunday afternoon when the brakes gave out on a hill in the middle of a major four-corner intersection. Don turned left, blasted the horn and plowed ahead, somehow landing us safely into the parking lot of our apartment complex. I told you he was cool under pressure. After this adventure, Uncle Bernie's car sat in the parking lot for a couple of years and became an attractive planter for many varieties of New Jersey weeds. It was an eye-catching focal point of our garden apartment complex.

We went to movies at the Palisades Park Theater for our weekly entertainment. Our most memorable film was *Sasquatch*, a narrated travelogue about Big Foot. For two hours the chase was experienced from a slanted and shaky camera angle. The audience never actually got to see Big Foot, only very large footprints. What did we care? We were young and in love.

On warm summer days, we met Don's grandfather at the Leonia pool across the street from our apartment complex. We sat with him and the seventy-year-old crowd. They usually watched the ladies in swimsuits and commented accordingly. Their lively conversations carried on throughout the luxurious summer afternoons. Don and I laughed contentedly as we stretched out soaking in the sun. It was a delightful way to spend the weekend.

Congregation Sons of Israel, a Conservative synagogue, was located directly across the street from our apartment building right next to the swim club. We had everything we needed a few feet away: religion and a community pool. During the High

Holidays of Rosh Hashanah and Yom Kippur, we attended services and for social activities, we joined the Young Couples Club.

I called the synagogue office one afternoon about setting up a meeting with the rabbi, and I spoke directly to his secretary. Since my married name was Armstrong and this was 1978, she did not mince words with me. She tersely said that since Donald was not Jewish, we could not be members of the synagogue. It was an unpleasant phone conversation. She preempted the rabbi, to whom I should have spoken to directly. I was young and hurt, but I didn't let it stop us from attending on the High Holidays or participating in the Young Couples Club with Don by my side.

In stark contrast to the secretary, long-standing members were gracious, kind, and welcoming to us. They made us feel at home whenever we entered the synagogue. We fondly remember their warm hospitality and acceptance of us as a new young couple.

There is something very unique about Judaism. It seeps deep into your soul and even if you were raised without a Jewish education, you maintain an ethnic identity. This is how it was for me. I needed to belong to a Jewish community on some level and Don instinctively understood this. He strongly supported our Jewish connections.

And here is what got interesting. We began our married lives celebrating Jewish holidays like Passover and Hanukkah. I also observed Rosh Hashanah and Yom Kippur, but I didn't know how to celebrate any others. We celebrated Christmas and Easter for Don, and we both attended synagogue on the High Holidays. Once while visiting with Grandmother Armstrong in North Carolina, we went to a Sunday church service with her. We were warmly welcomed there too. We did just fine with this arrangement. I have to admit that I was not thrilled the first time we brought a Christmas tree into the apartment. I grew up believing that Jews were not allowed to celebrate Christmas. It was the big no-no.

Although never being 100 percent comfortable with it, I did my best and we had wonderful Christmas celebrations with Don's family. I liked the idea of giving to someone you love to please them. I enjoyed seeing the look of surprise as they opened their gifts. It was in this spirit of giving that I celebrated the holiday. I was doing something important for Don and his family. Don had been so terrific about accepting Judaism in our lives. We went on this way for nine years—until something happened. We moved to our first home in Ridgewood, New Jersey, and joined the Conservative synagogue.

Two: I Didn't Die

I was not born a perfect child. I had a hole in my heart called a VSD, ventricular septal defect. Sometimes, as an unborn baby's heart is forming, the large wall between the right and left sides of the heart does not close completely. This wall is called the septum. If the septum has a hole in it between the ventricles, the problem is called a ventricular septal defect. In some cases, if the hole is small, it closes naturally as the child matures. If the hole does not close naturally, it needs to be repaired surgically. Since the hole in my heart did not close, my parents were faced with the prospect of experimental open-heart surgery to save their daughter. Nonetheless, I lived a cheerful childhood without showing any real signs of my illness until my fourth birthday, when I began to slow down.

Doctor Louis Krafchik, our local pediatrician in New Brunswick, diagnosed my illness when I was an infant. He told my mother that I would need surgery in order to survive. Otherwise, as I grew older, I would become more and more tired and then eventually die. The doctor hoped that by the time I needed the surgery, the medical technology would be available to save my life.

My mother, Lillian, was young and beautiful in the 1950s. She had one healthy daughter, my sister, Bobbie. I was her second, "imperfect" child. My beloved Aunt Mary described me as a pretty blond baby with bright blue eyes. I remember many afternoons looking up and watching Aunt Mary bustle around her kitchen while I lay on her spotlessly clean floor, contently drinking my bottle of milk. I lived in a protected, loving environment.

My mother's four older sisters doted on our family. Out of the five sisters (Mary, Rose, Jennie, Katie, and Lillian) three were married and had children. The cousins grew up together as close as brothers and sisters; it was Martin, Bobbie, Amy, Sandy, and Lois in that birth order. The sisters spoke Yiddish on the phone to each other and to Ida, our grandmother, when they didn't want us to understand what they were saying. To this day, I wish I had learned the language. Out of the five cousins, I was the sick one.

My parents contacted Deborah Hospital and spoke to a wonderful Hospital Superintendent named Clara Franks. Clara agreed to let me undergo the experimental procedure, and it would be free of charge. To this day, Deborah Hospital does not bill the patient or family for hospitalization or surgery. It remains an oasis of hope and charity. Only with the creation of medical insurance was the hospital reimbursed by any means other than donations. In 1959, my parents could not have afforded the hospital bill that amounted to $25,000 dollars.

Doctor Charles Bailey did my operation. He had successfully performed the first open heart surgery at Deborah on July 28, 1958, on William Demartino, a little three-year-old boy. My surgery followed eight months later on March 23, 1959, when I was five years old. The blood in my body kept circulating during the surgery with the help of the newly developed heart-lung machine. Before the operation and during recovery, I remember playing, laughing, and enjoying my fragile childhood in the comfort of Deborah Hospital's warm embrace.

This April 22, 1959 excerpt from *The Jewish Journal* describes my surgery:

> A little five-year-old girl will live! Her open heart miraculously mended because of the hearts of others. Little Sandra 'Sandy' Zimmerman, daughter of Myron and Lillian Zimmerman of

115 South Third Avenue, Highland Park, New Jersey will play with her friends once more because of the wonders of modern surgery and the love and heart of the Deborah Hospital at Browns Mills. Through the efforts of the New Brunswick Chapter of Deborah, Lillian Zimmerman contacted Mrs. Clara Franks, Hospital Superintendent, at Browns Mills who set the wheels in motion. All facilities were thrown open to the distraught parents and everything possible was done to speed the child on the long road to cure and recovery. Charles P. Bailey, internationally known heart surgeon and Chairman of Deborah's medical board, agreed to perform the operation when Sandy was medically ready. Then the moment was at hand Sandy's 'D' Day—her day of deliverance. She was prepared early Monday morning, March 23, for the operation and Doctor Bailey and his remarkable staff of doctors proceeded. It was touch and go—every move a vital one, every motion a step toward life or death. Hours passed ever so slowly and the miracle went on...then as the fourth hour was about to come to a close and after 'Sandy' had been aided by the heart-lung machine for a period of sixty-seven minutes, it was over—surgery completed, half the battle accomplished, but just half as 'Sandy' was now to enter the danger period of the post-operative recovery stage. For four days and nights a doctor, two nurses and a nurse's aide slept by her bedside, keeping a 24-hour-a-day watch. For days, everyone prayed for the little child and her parents. Friends, throughout Highland Park and New Brunswick anxiously asked each other, 'How's Sandy?'... No news was forthcoming...'Sandy' with her parents by her side, was waging her own personal battle...all that could be done had been done. Only 'Sandy' could do the job with God's help. And then the miracle came...the announcement...'Patient out of danger—recovery in sight.'

The good news is that you already know the outcome. I survived as a testament to Deborah Hospital's continuing success story—a thriving example of human expertise and compassion. Large donations of blood and love saved my life.

Why didn't I die? I knew that I had a 50/50 chance at life or death. I was a child, but I wasn't ignorant. I was shocked one day when I overheard the doctor telling my mother the grim facts: "The operation has a 50 percent success rate," he said. "If we don't do the surgery, she will die within the year."

I remember lying on the gurney and saying a final goodbye to my mother. Her grief overwhelmed me. What did I comprehend at five? I was happy, but I thought how little I knew about life. I had lived for five years, and if I were to die, what would I miss? What would my future be like? I was not old enough to imagine what lay ahead. I understood that this could be the end. I wanted to live for my mother.

As I lay on the operating table, I prayed. Although not having much knowledge of God, I instinctively knew somehow that a greater good existed. I had nowhere else to turn. To my right and my left stood doctors and nurses while scary man-made equipment loomed over my head—men, women, and machinery that would save my life. *If I could live, God, then my mother won't have to suffer. My death will destroy her. What would become of her, if I were to die?* It was a child's cry of love for my mother because that was the deepest love I knew. My voice was heard and my prayers were answered. As I drifted off to sleep with the anesthesia, I did not go into the operation alone. I was not put to sleep until I knew that I would live. How is that possible? I cannot explain it, but God answered my prayers. My mother's presence sustained me through my illness, surgery, and recovery. Her love and devotion caused me to seek life.

During my hospital stay, I was content and secure despite the severity of the situation. Due to the wisdom of the hospital policy, my mother lived in the same room with me the entire time. With their support, she was able to handle my illness. Her strength depended on Deborah's philosophy of partnership with the parent for the full recovery of the child. At the same time, we experienced an immeasurable amount of kindness as good men and women surrounded us. Two weeks before the operation and two weeks after, we were treated like royalty. I have fond memories of catching rides on the back of dinner carts, waving to patients while a nurse wheeled the meals and me along. I entered the hospital deathly ill, but I was never too weak to relish the attention. Doctors, nurses, and volunteers met all our needs and showered us with love and affection. "A child without the security of someone she loves with her is a poor risk in the operating room," insisted Clara Franks, a very wise hospital superintendent.

My surgery took its toll on my mother. When I was out of danger, the emotional trauma triggered my mother's mental breakdown. The floodgates were opened to all those feelings that she had been keeping in check. She was hospitalized, given shock treatment, and in and out of psychiatrist offices throughout the rest of my childhood. Although my aunts had assured me that there had been signs of her illness before my surgery, I believe the trauma triggered her unending battle with mental illness. Friendships were hard for my parents to keep because we never knew when my mother would "go off." My mother died of a stroke in 1992 at the age of sixty-eight.

On December 9, 2002, ten years after her death, while on an overnight visit to Deborah Hospital to celebrate its eightieth anniversary, I overcame the emotional trauma of my mother's mental illness. I remembered a time buried in my past. As I approached the familiar hospital walkway, I became that scared five-year-old little girl, so many years ago. I wore my fancy gray overcoat with the black velvet collar and matching pillbox hat. I clung innocently to my mother as we walked hand-in-hand into the hospital that would determine my life or death. Overwhelmed by strong memories, I timidly entered the same building that I had slept in as a child with my mother on a cot beside me. I was a grown woman now with three children of my own. I could just imagine how hard my surgery was on my mother—all those nights she slept beside me, not knowing if I would live or die.

That evening, I plopped down on the floor to record my speech for the following morning's celebration. I was hit by a wave of pure, childlike happiness. For a split second, all the layers of heartache wore away and I was a child playing on the floor in my hospital room, completely content. Where was this coming from? The familiarity of the hospital room with memories of being happy with my mother came back to me, but then her unfortunate breakdown caused me to toss and turn in bed through the night. Finally, I began to cry:

It was because I was imperfect. It was because of my illness. I caused you to live your life in a personal hell. It was my fault that you were never the same. I thought that when I prayed to God to allow me to live that you would be fine after the surgery, because I was granted life. If I hadn't been born with a hole in my heart, you would have lived a stable, happy life.

I sensed her comforting me—soothing me. *It wasn't your fault that I was ill. You cannot blame yourself anymore. It wasn't your fault. I am at peace now. You must be at peace too.*

It hurt so much and yet I was relieved to finally let it out. I was reliving the pain, her pain and mine. When I awoke the next morning, I visualized her as forever young, confident, and beautiful, the way she appeared when I was five years old, before my surgery and during my hospital stay. The mental illness that ruined her was gone. She was vibrant, strong, and happy. This is how I will always remember her.

Now, I could go about my life to the best of my ability, no longer walking on eggshells, afraid of imperfection. I felt immediate relief from the burden of her illness. I was not to blame. I did not have to be perfect in order to live successfully. I had renewed strength to face the future in a more powerful way without guilt. I was ready to be someone else, someone better.

My speech at the anniversary celebration highlighted Doctor Charles Bailey, the world-renowned surgeon who saved my life. He was a pioneer in his field. He believed that surgery could be performed on the heart like any other muscle in the body. One tranquil spring afternoon in 1993 while my family visited the Smithsonian History and Technology Museum in Washington, D.C., I suddenly looked down and found myself staring at medical instruments that Doctor Bailey had used during his early heart operations. These medical instruments were used to save my life! Shortly after this trip, I contacted Doctor Bailey. I hoped there was time left to thank him for all he had done for me. Fortunately, Doctor Bailey lived a long full life, and he responded to my letter.

Dear Sandy,
Thank you so much for your lovely letter. Your happy life with your husband and three children makes an older doctor (I am 82 years old) feel that he was of some good after all... Of course, Deborah is a wonderful place. Just imagine how many people they have helped...As to yourself, I am confident that the hole in your heart is thoroughly closed, healed over. It will never trouble you again. Too bad I couldn't tell your mother that. It might have helped her...Do help Deborah whenever you can. It is one of the great health centers of America—perhaps the world.
My very warmest wishes,
Charles P. Bailey

The amount of blood necessary for my operation was thirty-five pints. My father's office staff at the New York Post generously donated enormous amounts of blood. The Jewish War Veterans had a busload of donors who were on call, ready and waiting. So much blood and love went into my survival.

Many years later, a gentleman called me upon hearing that my dad was seriously ill. After his questions concerning my father's health, he remarked, "You don't remember me, but I donated blood for you forty-two years ago." Suddenly, at that moment, I was hit by the full realization that hundreds of strangers had donated their blood for my survival. I don't know them and I can't personally thank them. It then occurred to me that my blood was not my own. Good-hearted men and women were responsible for the blood that pumps through my veins. After all these years, I still do not know where my blood begins and their blood ends. I am a living, breathing testament to their compassion.

With today's medical technology, a child usually stays in the hospital twenty-four hours to patch a hole like mine. I remained at Deborah for a month. Thirty-five pints of blood were needed for my surgery and now only one or two pints are necessary. This operation is no longer life threatening. The progress, the modernization, and medical miracles continue at a rapid pace. However, the need for hope, charity, and love remains unchanged.

Deborah Hospital teaches the art of giving, an art form that instructs others how to give back to humanity. We are all artists in life, and giving to others is one of the most creative and beneficial art forms in existence today. It all began at Deborah with the premise of its dynamic founder, Dora Moness Shapiro: "There is no price on life." The hospital was established so that patients and their families were given the benefits of hospital care without a fee. And it remains the same today as unconditional love still permeates its halls. A moment in the hospital chapel reinforces the sense of peace derived from helping someone in need. Deborah continues to reach out to people regardless of race, creed, or religion. Each life is valued and saved, one at a time. All strangers are welcomed like family. I was once a stranger there, yet my parents paid nothing and I received life.

Three: I Can't Read Hebrew

Don said, "Since we live in Ridgewood, we should check out a local congregation." I took his suggestion and arranged a meeting with Rabbi Noam Marans in his private study with Zachary (age six) and Tammie (age three) in tow. The rabbi was a youthful, energetic twenty-six-year-old and we were in our early thirties. He looked rather nice and not scary at all. Would this rabbi kick us out because we had fallen in love? Would he lecture us about what was already a done deal? How would he react to us as an interfaith couple? Would he let us join his Conservative congregation? Rabbi Marans welcomed us, encouraged us, and calmly spoke to us about our future at Temple Israel. From that moment on, our lives changed forever.

The rabbi informed us that the entire family would be considered members. It wasn't me coming in as the member with Don as my guest. This made an enormous difference to our feelings of acceptance in a Conservative congregation. We told Rabbi Marans that the children would be raised in the Jewish faith and that we wanted to do this as a partnership. He was pleased. For the first time, since we were married, I felt (religiously) like a million bucks. I had married a man I loved and on top of it all, after nine years, the rabbi didn't yell at us. I am making a joke, but in all seriousness, he could have turned us away and our lives would not be as wonderful as they are today. The only parting comment he had for Donald was, "I will encourage your conversion, but I will never think less of you if you don't convert." We found a wise rabbi.

Our congregation became our home away from home. We immersed ourselves in the synagogue and raised our children in a happy, supportive environment. Members of all ages mingled and our children experienced the best in people, both young and old. As we became part of this dynamic community, our participation rapidly increased. Don and I were grateful to be accepted as an interfaith couple.

When I was pregnant with Tiffany, our third child, Donald said to me, "You take the Hebrew 101 course. Since we will be raising our children in the Jewish faith, you need to learn Hebrew. Most of the prayers are in Hebrew and you need to know them. You take the first course, and I will take it the second time it is offered." I was adamant in my reply: "I don't want to take this Hebrew course. I never liked learning a new language, and I'm not very good at it." A week later, I signed up for the course. Don was true to his word and took the class a year after me.

Hebrew 101 consisted of six women in a weekly class with the rabbi. Our text was a book called *Shalom Aleichem* by Noah Golinkin. Years later I met Rabbi Golinkin and had the unique opportunity to hear about his teaching method firsthand (I wish I had known this fact while I was struggling through the lessons). I was self-conscious and the worst in my class. I disliked reading out loud in front of everyone else, and I felt like I was back in first grade, afraid and on the spot. To avoid embarrassment, I studied over and over again from our weekly practice tapes. The point of our Hebrew text was to develop letter and word recognition with each letter building into a word and each new word filling a place in the prayer. Every page brought us closer to learning the Friday night prayer, "Shalom Aleichem."

During class one evening, Rabbi Marans turned to me and commented, "Considering your background, you are doing remarkably well." That's all I needed to hear since a little encouragement goes a long way. I began to pursue my study with a passion. Later,

I would tell my own students: "Ten minutes a day is all you need to learn Hebrew, just be conscientious and study consistently. Find time to practice as you wait to pick your children up from school, between carpools, or during your lunch hour at work. Fit it into your day and you'll be amazed at what you will accomplish."

I learned to really enjoy reading Hebrew as I grew more and more confident each passing week. I began the course in February, and by May, I was leading parts of the Friday night service at a Camp Ramah retreat weekend in the Berkshires. If someone had said to me, Sandy, you will do this, I would never have believed it. But I did do it.

I remember the day when we drove up to our first Camp Ramah retreat with Tiffany, our newborn, in an infant seat alongside her brother and sister who sang and played around in the back of the van. We were packed to the brim with stuff that included all those items that were absolutely necessary for a weekend away with an infant, a toddler, and a young boy. Don also filled up the car with various music paraphernalia and several guitars for the evening campfire sing-along.

We piled into the overstuffed car for the two-hour ride. The radio was blasting rock music (our rule is whoever drives gets to choose the radio station). I simply put on my earphones and listened to my tape of the Friday night service. I was unusually uptight and it was hard to focus on the service with the rock music and children singing along in the background. But as I continued to progress in my studies, I learned to ignore the distractions and go for my goal. Often in my congregational involvement, I put aside the smaller points in order to get to the bigger picture. Laundry piled up on the bedroom floor but I overlooked it, stood at the foot of my bed, and practiced. The clutter in my life did not matter, the goals did.

After we arrived at Camp Ramah and got settled in our rustic cabin, I led a portion of the Friday night service. Although I did not comprehend exactly what I was saying, I expected to learn its meaning in time. I entered a whole new world of lay leadership that evening. The leap from knowing nothing, to leading a prayer service in a few months, astounded me. This motivated me to become more active in all aspects of our congregational life. I wanted to share my newly acquired gifts with others.

As the years progressed, one of my volunteer jobs was to take potential Hebrew readers into my home for free, private lessons. Several people couldn't make it to the evening classes at the synagogue. My flexibility allowed students to learn at different times of the day. I instructed many adults to read Hebrew using the same text that I used to learn Hebrew, *Shalom Aleichem*. A few students wanted to brush up on reading skills twenty years after their Bar or Bat Mitzvah (Jewish boys/girls coming of age ceremony) and others started without any prior knowledge. I taught each one of them individually in my home, in their home, over the phone, or while having coffee in town. A few wished to make it up to the bimah (platform from which the Torah is read) for an aliyah (a Hebrew honor at the Torah). I tailored the lessons to meet their needs, which was a key element to their success. In this highly individualized society, people want their religious goals to be met quickly and efficiently. When requests are addressed in a respectful, personal manner, miracles happen.

During one Saturday morning, I looked up in amazement as I heard one of my students chant from the Torah. I was moved to tears because I remembered when Anne initially arrived at my door—afraid and quite unsure of herself. I encouraged her to practice and after a few weeks, she had absorbed enough to read Hebrew well. In four months, she walked out of my house fully confident. Torah study provided a necessary uplift, as well as a springboard into her Jewish identity. She felt a connection between past, present, and future generations, uniting thousands of years of Jewish ancestry.

It didn't take Anne long to achieve proficiency while practicing a small amount of time each day. All it required was determination and help from an enthusiastic guide. She became a better Torah reader than her teacher! I was glad to be there for her when she needed the help. Several of my students surpassed my knowledge. Once they got started, they just kept going. It was their spiritual journey that mattered, not mine. To attract additional students, I placed advertisements in the synagogue's newsletters. Here is an excerpt:

> Are you tired of mumbling "matzah farfel, matzah farfel" under your breath while you are pretending to read Hebrew prayers? The tunes are familiar, but you need to know—What page are we on? Where are we on the page? What's considered a solo for the Cantor and what's not? Why are we reading prayers in Hebrew anyway? In other words, I need help, but I feel like my questions are stupid.

These ads were effective for congregants who were on the verge of asking for help, but too frightened to begin.

Several years later, I had the pleasure of meeting the author of *Shalom Aleichem* at a synagogue convention in 2002 called *Five Pillars of Conservative Judaism*. One afternoon during the convention, I attended a session on Jewish education. I piped up when the group leader asked, "At what point in your adult education did you feel like you turned a major corner?" I told the group that I learned everything through my beginning Hebrew course with Noah Golinkin's *Shalom Aleichem*. It was this book that opened the door to Judaism for me. The group laughed, and of course, I didn't know why. I felt quite embarrassed and thought I had said something terribly wrong. I asked timidly, "What's so funny?" They told me that the author, Rabbi Golinkin, was sitting right next to me! I was pleasantly surprised and giggled in disbelief.

During the precious time that I spent with Rabbi Golinkin, he shared his Hebrew literacy campaign strategy. He was passionate about the entire congregation learning Hebrew. Rabbi Golinkin established several nights a week of adult education. If one night was inconvenient, then another night might be better. There were no excuses to delay attending since the course was offered consecutively throughout the week. The rabbi's persistent method was successful when almost all of his congregants learned Hebrew. Here are some words of advice that Rabbi Golinkin gave me: "Young people today need to take passion and do great things with it." I thought this to be sound advice from another wise rabbi.

Four: A Day to Rest

Shabbat changed us. Every Friday night at sundown until sundown the following Saturday night, Don and I slowly adjusted our lifestyle and adopted the weekly Shabbat (Sabbath) rituals and celebrations. We were taught how to recite the prayers for lighting the candles. We learned the blessings for our children, the wine, and the meal. We implemented our newfound knowledge at home and created Shabbat together. It was a creation because it required incremental steps of choice, will power, and persistence. The anticipation of Shabbat impacted our entire home throughout the week of preparation, food shopping, and cooking. Shabbat is the day when we took a break from our busy schedules and relished life.

What is unique about this time in our lives? How did it become so important? After all, I did not celebrate Shabbat with my parents and Don was not raised in the Jewish faith. What compelled us to become observant? It was the peaceful feeling we sought from entering a spiritual realm once a week in an attempt to reach a heightened level of holiness in our home. When the candles were lit and the children gathered around, tranquility infused our lives. The Hebrew prayers came slowly at first, and the blessings were awkward transliterations. It took a while for the prayers to be chanted smoothly and even longer to gain comprehension. But, no matter how flawed our rituals were initially, it was a mitzvah (commandment) to rest on the seventh day and celebrate Shabbat to the best of our abilities.

Don rarely joined us at the Friday night dinner table due to his work demands. Often, I was left alone with the children to do the rituals, make dinner, and see that they behaved. Although Don wanted to be at dinner, he worked on Wall Street where leaving work early to be home with your family was not the accepted norm. Nonetheless, I loved this Friday night celebration.

Shabbat impacted the entire week. By Wednesday, planning for the weekend menu was already in progress. It was easier to prepare a few days ahead of time so that Friday would not be so hectic. I longed for the house to look nice at candle lighting with the rooms picked up and neat. I wanted the cooking to be done and ready. Unfortunately, what I wanted was not always what I got. It took many years to reach the point where occasionally, before candle lighting, I could walk around the house and say, "I feel caught up. I'm ready." It was a rare but welcome occurrence.

The feeling of Shabbat spilled over into Saturday. Don was able to sleep and get the rest he needed before another week on Wall Street. Saturday turned into a complete day of rest (I didn't bug him to do household chores or go shopping). This brought an amazing amount of peace into our lives. Restful afternoons were spent taking long naps on my favorite Shabbat couch. It had a sign on it that said, "Don't bother me!" (I wished). Meal preparations were done in advance so kitchen work was nonexistent. I read Jewish texts in order to savor them at least one day a week. Shabbat was a method of "just being there" for my husband, my children, and me.

It took years of little changes to allow us to indulge in a full day of rest. But the more we did it, the better our lives became. The more joy we experienced on this day, the happier we were during the week. This peaceful oasis in our lives kept the remainder of the week glued together. Like pieces of a puzzle, Shabbat was the seventh piece that fit right into the middle of the board, aligning our priorities. This special day was a grounding force, and a chance to plug into renewed spiritual energy.

We began the Shabbat dinner ritual in the dining room. This proved to be too physically taxing for me with the children, so I eventually opted for the kitchen. One particular Shabbat experience stands out in my mind. It was a typical Friday night at the kitchen table with a white tablecloth, a bottle of Manischewitz wine, and a newly baked challah. That evening the children were unusually silly. I was frustrated. Enough was enough. After I had worked so hard to put out this lovely meal for them, they were acting wild and not appreciating it. So I announced, "This is it, I have had it! No more Shabbat dinners! You do not know how to behave." My ten-year-old son turned to me calmly and said, "You should not punish God because we are misbehaving." We went on with the meal and I never threatened to take Shabbat away again. Silliness, teasing, and an inability to sit still were not the issues, Shabbat was. Throughout the unending joking with his sisters, Zachary knew why we were all sitting at the Friday night table and the importance of this ritual. He was too young to sit still, but not too young to understand.

As children, they were mine to direct on Friday evenings, which meant I gladly eliminated television after the candles were lit. This encouraged them to interact with each other during their formative years. Often the evenings resulted in massive blanket-pillow tents that our youngest, Tiffany, would crawl in and out of, and sometimes get lost inside. They often played hide-and-seek with the neighborhood children who had just finished sharing our Shabbat meal. Despite their gender and age differences, the siblings and their friends learned how to play together. I knew it would be better for them to use their imaginations in creative play. Learning to communicate with each other was key to their social and spiritual development.

Shutting off the television one night a week was probably the best thing I ever did. They learned how to be together without electronic interference. Occasionally, during our meal, I would remind them of the necessity of always looking out for each other. I told them that Dad and I wouldn't be around forever. As they grew up, the sibling rivalries, jealousies, and internal fighting were minimal. They were kind to each other, not perfect, but not a problem either. They remain good friends today.

One Shabbat when Zachary was a senior in high school, Tammie was a freshman, and Tiffany was a sixth grader, I sat at the Friday night dinner table and cried. Three teenagers (all going through the "uppity stage") were too much for me. I usually had a break when they took turns being difficult, but this time I was having a hard time with all of them. Before Shabbat began, I wrote down on index cards what I would like each one of them to change, and I handed them their list. They thought this was funny, but since verbal communication was no longer working, I thought the written word might help.

As I handed out their cards, I broke down in tears. They overwhelmed me and I spilled it out at the dinner table. If I was this upset on Shabbat, my favorite day of the week, then their misbehavior was getting to me! They took the cue and snapped out of it. Afterward, our lives were much better. They hadn't realized how much they were hurting me until we sat down together and discussed it. Funny how this episode paralleled the earlier one when they were much younger. On both occasions, they upset me with their misbehavior and evoked similar emotions. The years in between didn't seem to matter. The observance of the Shabbat dinner withstood time and maintained its healing power throughout the course of our family life.

Shabbat was critical to our evolving Jewish identities. We stopped one day a week and thanked God for our blessings including each other. It worked, and it worked regardless of who was at the dinner table. The key was that we were consistent and we observed the tradition to the best of our ability. Week after week, month after month, year after year, we strived to maintain the Sabbath. I learned through this ritual observance that spiritual growth will evolve, only if and when you start. Where religion is concerned, not everything is black or white and many gray areas exist. It is within these gray areas that the right path is found to observance. A person could be easily overwhelmed by the enormity of it all, yet by taking small steps, religious life blooms. Broken down into modest pieces, religious practice becomes cumulative, inviting, unthreatening, and very rewarding.

An Exquisite Day

Life is not the same for one day. The workweek stops including sorting mail, returning phone calls, paying bills, and shopping (I was the purchasing agent for our home). We relax, read, sleep, congregate with our fellow synagogue members, and study Torah. We love to play "catch up" with our friends during the Kiddush—the festive meal after services. We relish the life in our body. The world is sharper, clearer because we are not trying to manipulate it. We exist, observe, and enjoy. We are there for God, and God is there for us.

Shabbat is the path to holiness. If we don't take a day to reflect, how can we attempt to bring holiness into our lives? Isn't this what we ultimately want? We are trying to prevail over the terror, violence, and profanity. How else can we achieve our loftier goals without the regular commitment to a day of thinking about higher ideals? When we become too busy, too engrossed in our stressful daily existence, it is too easy to forget about this day to rest. As we scurry around, it is hard to remember what is important and what is not. We cannot seem to catch our breath during the workweek. Sometimes we even cut short our family vacations, the most precious time of all, because we are thinking about work and are too busy to iron out our personal relationships. We rush around from one obligation to the next trying to stay ahead of the game. But what game are we talking about? Is it the game of life, the commitment to live a good, holy life? We work hard to provide for our children and our family, but we often forget the underlying reason for this effort. Do we see a greater plan, a way of creating a better, more spiritually enriched world for our future generations?

Without Shabbat, all days are the same. Nothing is distinct. Separations between the holy and the profane, or even the mundane and extraordinary, do not exist. One day runs into the next and we are not evolving as God intended. We are little more than animals going from one moment to the next, never appreciating the wonder and grandeur of our lives.

A Time Alone with God

Shabbat became my time alone with God—as a parent to a child. God would give me the unconditional love and direction that I needed. As much as possible, I said no to outside interference because I understood the precious nature of this gift of time and reflection. I marveled that I survived a hole in my heart and continued to thrive. I prayed for the prosperity and growth of our synagogue, along with the health and welfare of our family. I prayed that one day my husband would be Jewish.

I learned through prayer that I was not greater or less than any other man or woman. I realized that we were all pretty much the same. Every person has the potential to do some good and to be better. Through prayer, the impossible, or what we originally thought to be impossible, can be achieved. There is a "burning bush" inside every one of us, keeping us alive. It is our eternal flame that is refueled on this day of rest.

Five: Kindness to Strangers

Welcoming strangers into our congregation became extremely important. We were losing the first generation that built the synagogue and we needed new blood to exist. It was the right time in my life to pitch in and help, so I created a welcoming committee to boost our membership numbers. We needed to grow educationally, economically, and socially. The only way to achieve significant growth was a large-scale new-member drive. I began by randomly calling people from real estate lists. Sometimes, even if one partner in the household wasn't Jewish, I discovered that the other one was. It was like fishing. I threw out my line, but never knew what might come up. Like a Jewish Welcome Wagon, I reached out to families new to the area and greeted them at synagogue events. The newest families in the area were the most eager to connect to others. It was always harder to engage them once they were already established in a neighborhood.

People reacted well to initial greetings and hospitality. For this reason, unaffiliated families usually remained on our mailing list for five to eight years. One particular family joined our congregation after being on the list for ten years. They placed their twin boys in our religious school and their mother joined the membership committee. A prospective member never gets tired of positive outreach. Consistent welcoming and kindness to a stranger ultimately pays off.

The more successful I was, the more aware I became of emotional voids. If it was so easy, in a few minutes a day, to reach out and connect with other people in a positive way, then why wasn't this type of community building being done more often? Welcoming others into a religious community covers all traditions, not just Judaism. A wealth of fundamental human goodness and productivity is out there waiting to be tapped. My success in recruiting new members was not necessarily due to my sales ability, but to the fact that my product, inclusion in a community, fulfilled a basic human need. I was persuasive, but a deeper chord was being struck. I did something differently, something other people were not taking the time to do. I actively pursued and sympathetically listened. In most cases, people were eager to participate, but they needed to be encouraged with an honest, heartfelt invitation.

Often, they were as disconnected as I once was. I understood their emptiness. I explained to them the beauty of religion as it played out in my life. They simply lacked a point of access so I offered them a solution. My conversations gave them direction. I wondered, how could something so basic be ignored? What stops us? We are technologically advanced, and yet we are not meeting our communal and spiritual needs. Why are there so many unhappy, disconnected people out there? Why are they not looking at religion for solace, guidance, comfort, and community?

People responded to my phone calls and they were eager to listen. My method seldom changed, and the responses were always similar. The key to getting people involved in a religious community is the personal approach. Forget about standardized letters because they get thrown out. A handwritten invitation to an event and a one-to-one conversation works best. People need the personal touch because they are often hesitant to introduce themselves. Approaching people in a kind, enthusiastic manner will make an immediate difference in their response and potential future involvement. Emailing is convenient, but it does not replace the necessary face-to-face contact to make lasting impressions.

A house of worship should look for a welcoming representative who loves the religious community and who is sensitive to the nature of recruitment. There is no miracle involved in religious participation. It takes minimal effort to extend kindness to others. The act of welcoming is a win-win situation. You win by having them become a part of your community. They win by finding a home and friends within their religious affiliation. The extra bonus happens when they come around full circle and actively recruit other families to join the congregation.

In our Conservative congregation, new recruits expanded their knowledge when they observed others become successful in areas of religious life. For instance, reading Hebrew was not initially a goal for many of the new members. By pointing out the incremental achievements of others, they were inspired to continue their own religious education. Many new members became ritually active participants because they saw other members read from the Torah. They were inspired by example. In addition, new members rose to presidential leadership positions on the Board of Directors, Men's Club, and Sisterhood. Interfaith couples found comfort zones as they observed other similar families enjoy synagogue life. An open atmosphere ultimately fostered several conversions. Religious education for individuals and families boomed. Children attended religious programs including Ramah summer camps. Some parents even placed their children into special Hebrew Day Schools.

Would you say these changes were small miracles of creation and regeneration? By setting examples, one person, or a small group of people, lead others down the path of religious participation. A domino effect expands religious involvement and achievement. It isn't hard to trigger an initial change in others. As more people become active, more people benefit. This is the beauty of community-based religion. One person positively thrives off the accomplishments of the other, and then it grows. The amount of welcoming done to achieve these goals was a drop in the bucket compared to the flood of success.

Welcoming Others With "Ruach"

> When God began to create heaven and earth—the earth being unformed and void, with darkness over the surface of the deep and a wind from God sweeping over the water—God said, "Let there be light"; and there was light. God saw that the light was good, and God separated the light from the darkness. (Genesis 1:1-4; Rabbinical 1999)

When God made the world, he did it with "ruach," the Hebrew word for "wind, breath, and spirit." Black holes are voids in the universe that parallel voids in our souls. A void existed, and then God created heaven and earth. God filled the void. He sparked light and life into his creation and said that it was good. Every soul is given the opportunity to continue the act of creation with a spark of personal goodness.

With "ruach" we fill spiritual voids. As people join congregations, it is their spiritual progress, their individual creation story that energizes all of us. Their participation enriches the community and gives it a vibrant glow. A spark of their personal energy becomes a ray of sunshine by eliminating black holes and increasing the "ruach" of the congregation. Every person counts when creating a religious community.

Six: Jumping Into Judaism

Our family jumped into religious life throughout the years of involvement with our congregation. A new holiday or ritual observance meant another opportunity to learn and experience Jewish life to its fullest. New observances were gradually added and made our evolving Jewish lifestyle an ongoing adventure.

Passover

It was a beautiful sunny day at a sidewalk cafe in town, one of those great spring days for eating lunch outside. My girlfriends and I were relaxing, enjoying the moment, until someone mentioned Passover. Panic set in, as our calm exterior was broken. Where should we start? What should we do? What are we not doing this very moment that needs to get done? We calmed each other down, and then quickly changed the subject.

It was a week later and my Pesach (Hebrew for Passover) preparations had begun. Why am I doing this? Why do I switch my kitchen over? Why do I pull out all these special dishes? I must be crazy! Slowly, I remembered what I had forgotten in one year. Passover is a process, like our lives. It doesn't happen overnight and it doesn't have to be perfect, it just "is."

I unpacked my pots, pans, and dishes with all the detailed labels that I put away so carefully the year before. It was as if another person had been kind enough to place it in order for me.

I was so glad to find a Pesach map on how to proceed. Over the next three days, I cleaned out the kitchen cabinets and thoroughly removed all the breadcrumbs (known as hametz). Hametz are leavened products that include forms of grains such as pasta and cereal. Then I replaced our supplies with unleavened Passover items including matzah. Every time another kitchen area was ready, I felt more complete, more in order.

The next step was to search for the hametz left around the house. Let's see—Zachary had to be called out from the basement, Tammie was at a party, Don was still at work, and Tiffany was ready. Does this sound like a typical family? By ten o'clock in the evening, we were ready. Secretly, I scattered pieces of bread around the den. The children anxiously fidgeted with their flashlights. We said the prayer before the search for hametz and off they went. As pieces of challah were picked up, they crumbled all over the newly cleaned carpet. Now I know that removing all the hametz out of your house and lives is futile! So what's the point? The point is to try. It's the effort that makes the difference in our lives. When God passes over us, he sees that we attempted to perfect our home, our community, and our world.

Passover, like Shabbat, is a time phenomenon. We take the time to change. We start with small steps inside our homes, but we hope to carry over these efforts to our outside endeavors. We connect to our past by understanding our lives in the present. Our hands break up matzah no differently than the hands of our ancestors leaving Egypt thousands of years before us. We are one and the same. Passover forces us to remember this.

The house is ready, the hametz is out, and the festival meal must be prepared. I'm cooking, cooking, and cooking but there isn't enough time. I still have to review the Haggadah so that the Seder will run smoothly. What am I going to do? This is when the family pitches in. You can go out to dinner as a family, go to a play, or even on a vacation, but nothing compares to going into the kitchen and preparing for the holiday. Tammie arranged the Seder plate and then Don, Tammie, and Tiffany made an apple cake. Zachary set up the table even better than I did the year before. Decorations were hung and the house hummed with activity. Our deadline arrived and we were done. Passover began and so did the rest of our lives.

Challah

Baking challah for our Friday evening meal is one of the most powerful customs that my family built into our Shabbat experience. I never imagined myself as a baker, but the ritual has become more than just baking bread.

I baked our monthly allotment of challah today. As I began to mix the ingredients, I thought of my friends who taught me how to bake challah from scratch. Johanna and Denise each instructed me in their own style, and I incorporated their methods into my own. While I mix the flour, water, eggs, oil, and sugar together, I remember the bond created by this important ritual. Whenever one of us bakes challah, we think of each other.

We knead, turn, and form the dough in our hands as we shape our Jewish lives. We connect with thousands of years of mixing flour and water to sustain our people. Ancestral hands guide us as we move to the rhythm of timeless molding. Today, we have the convenience of purchasing bags of flour from the grocery store, and using measuring spoons, bowls, and nonstick pans. Some of us use bread makers to mix the flour. We are modernized, but we are forever connected to the past.

We sculpt the dough, just as we sculpt our families. Maneuvering the flour and water is the physical representation of our ability to nurture and form others. When my hands are thick into it, I think about how God is also shaping my life into lovely strains of braided dough ready to be baked.

While we prepare, we remember our ancestral redemption. The Jews who fled Egypt faced uncertainty and fear. Where were they going and how would they survive? In a hurry to leave, they left with matzah, the unleavened bread of affliction. They trusted

God and Moses to deliver them from Egyptian enslavement and Pharaoh's wrath.

Challah is our bread of freedom. Why? The dough must rise, and after it is kneaded, it is left to rise again. This process takes several hours to complete. No slave has the time or freedom to do this. Now, God allows us the blessing of dough rising. We toss, we play, and we move the flour around to the music of freedom in our lives. The dough sticks to our fingers. This physical bonding is nothing more than God clinging to our lives, holding on to us, and allowing us the freedom to honor those who came before us.

Sukkot

Our first Sukkot in New Jersey was celebrated on a cold, starry night in the synagogue's sukkah eating a warm, delicious meal with family and friends. During Sukkot, we are instructed to live in a temporary shelter (sukkah) like our ancestors who wandered in the desert for forty years. In our sukkah, we think about the transient nature of our lives and celebrate Israel's harvest season. Sukkot is like a Jewish Thanksgiving.

Our rabbi encouraged us to observe this special holiday in our home. Donald and Rabbi Marans went out early one morning to Paterson to obtain the skah, the greenery for the roof of our first sukkah. I remember their pleasure at successfully obtaining more greenery than we would ever need. This was the beginning of our Sukkot holiday experience.

During Yom Kippur services, I always think about the upcoming festival of Sukkot. What will Sukkot be like? Will we enjoy ourselves as much as last year? Will my husband build the sukkah in time? We sometimes build it just before the holiday begins. This year would be especially trying because our backyard was a heap of dirt due to construction. I was not sure if we could put up a sukkah at all. The loss of the holiday in its entire splendor would be difficult.

We went shopping for materials to build our first model of a sukkah out of cinder blocks for the base, wood, and cotton sheets. We switched to the larger, prefab tent version a few years later. We went with the deluxe model since our family had grown and needed more room to entertain our many guests. Our sukkah accommodated Girl Scout meetings including hilarious campouts and lunchtime visits from local elementary school classes. Favorite nights in the sukkah featured kosher Chinese food or Italian night with pizza. There were special evenings with candlelit Shabbat dinners.

The best part of the sukkah was the company. Rekindling friendships, family get-togethers, inviting synagogue members over at a time of loss or need, birthday celebrations, Hebrew literacy lessons, new and old neighbors dropping in to say hello, all brought us enjoyment during this holiday season. We understood that this fun included being commanded by God to live in the sukkah for the week. When we built our first sukkah, there were only three in our community, but eventually the number grew to over thirty. This holiday establishes the Jewish idea of fun and good cheer. We ate and drank like kings and queens, as if the world was created for our enjoyment.

One of my favorite activities is sleeping outdoors in a sukkah, under the stars. I wonder (as I do every year) why am I sleeping down on the hard ground when Don is in a warm, soft bed inside the house? Well, to do it, is to love it. This is when you feel the most connected to the holiday and the most vulnerable. I never closed my eyes without feeling the enormity of the universe surrounding me.

The store-bought cloth and wood materials of the sukkah offer a false sense of security, like the walls of our more established homes. Building materials surround us, but they will not bring us the comfort we seek. We have few possessions inside the newly constructed temporary dwelling. Yet, possessions seem small and insignificant compared to the beauty of the world around us in the still of the night. And yes, in these quiet moments in our sukkah, God's presence offers us the protection that no man-made structure ever will or can.

Keeping Kosher

Our involvement with our congregation centered on hosting events in our home, including dinners with our rabbi's family with cold kosher food on paper plates. I wanted our lives to reflect the sanctity of the shul (Yiddish for synagogue). The observance of Jewish dietary laws was a necessary step in this sanctification.

I diligently researched the possibility of keeping a kosher home. My rabbi recommended two books, *The Dietary Laws* by Samuel Dresner, Seymour Siegel, and David Pollock and *The Jewish Dietary Laws: Sanctify Life* by James Lebeau. The more I read about keeping kosher, the more it made sense.

A ladder of observance is presented in *The Jewish Dietary Laws.* Each rung of the ladder brings you closer to your goal. It appeared to be very methodical, but not something I would attempt to accomplish overnight. I did not come from an observant home. In fact, we sometimes ate sliced ham sandwiches for lunch and pork chops for dinner. The closest we came to kosher food was our Sunday morning breakfast when my Dad bought bagels and lox on the wings (salmon with the fins) from the local butcher.

As I became more educated in kashrut (Jewish religious dietary laws), I stopped to check what silverware I last used for what purpose. Had it been meat or dairy? This can get you nutty, after a while. Also, I poured over the Leviticus chapter in the Torah describing those animals that are permitted for consumption and those that are forbidden. The Torah continually teaches us to separate the holy from the profane. What struck me the most was the emphasis on the sanctity of life. Our heritage teaches us to balance the uncritical kindness, goodness, and life in mother's milk with the inevitable opposite—death. Meat symbolizes a sacrifice, a death in order that humans can sustain their lives. I felt strongly that dairy and meat must be separated in our home. Life and death are opposites; therefore, what we eat must be similarly divided.

How we consume food, in the commonness of our kitchens, reflects our view of life. There is no better way to show this reverence than in an "everyday" kitchen. By sanctifying our homes through kashrut, we continually recognize a higher spiritual order. We mirror the warmth of God's light, which pulsates throughout our home. Just as we light the Shabbat candles weekly, with kashrut we light up our lives everyday. Every trip to the butcher, every time we buy a kosher product, and at every meal we are reminded of the sanctity of life. The ordinary act of eating in our home is elevated to a religious experience.

After keeping kosher for several years, I took on the responsibility of kashering the homes of several synagogue members. Following the lead of my friend Rabbi Amy Roth—who honored me with a festive "kosher kitchen shower"—I taught others how to kasher their kitchens. When a member of the congregation was interested, I arranged a consultation. Each home was different. We made several lists of to-do, to-buy, and to-ask the rabbi. I gave them copies of the kashrut books to help answer their questions. I asked them to go through their kitchen supplies and think of meat or dairy. How might they envision the separation? They went through their refrigerator and pantry, slowly replacing non-kosher items with kosher ones.

Occasionally, we took a field trip and went on tours of kosher stores. I checked back in a few weeks to monitor their progress, answer questions, and work out a future plan of action. Questions were addressed like: How is your color scheme different for meat and dairy? What kitchen supplies can be saved and made kosher? They would pile up their newly acquired kitchenware and slowly put "used items" on hold for potential kashering.

Finally, the big day arrived and we "boiled up" for six to seven hours. Several large pots of boiling water were used to immerse and purify utensils, silverware, and cookware. Whatever could be saved in the original kitchen was saved and then kashered that day. The labor was intense but exciting, and two or three of us accomplished the task in one day. The real joy was walking out of a sparkling, newly kashered kitchen ready for a family to sanctify it with their presence.

Kosher Mistakes

Over the past few weeks, my family couldn't find a dairy knife, spoon, or fork in the kitchen. So I said, that's it, I have to open up the "drawer of mistakes" and kasher them. Over the past year, we had collectively made so many errors that we were almost out of utensils. I boiled up the water and began to kasher the silverware. I counted not ten, or twenty, but fifty-five mistakes! How could one family make so many errors? I laughed and remembered what family we were talking about (there were probably even more mistakes). Now, we have the necessary dairy utensils, but our lives are still not perfect, only better. I believe through Jewish practice that's the best we can do. The more rituals we participate in, the better we are. It's not always important that we do them perfectly; it's that we try our best. Striving to improve is our ultimate goal. Through religious observance, we attempt to eliminate chaos and restore order in our lives.

Wrapping Tefillin

"Take your soul on vacation" is exactly what I did for five days. I lived, breathed, and walked through history at the Jewish Theological Seminary (JTS) in Manhattan. I was part of the Wagner Institute, which is a lay leadership seminar established to create closer ties between synagogue members and the seminary. I was in a group of thirty people from across the country gathered together for a week of intensive Jewish education. As I soaked up our faith within the walls of the seminary, I was struck by the strong commitment of the students to their religious studies. Our future rabbis and teachers demonstrated a true passion for their religion. JTS is a safe environment to live and breathe Judaism with unlimited accessibility. The Wagner Institute for the layperson takes your soul on vacation and expands your Jewish imagination.

A profound result of my JTS experience was a new appreciation of what it means to be Jewish. I was given the opportunity to explore Judaism in ways that I never thought would be accessible to me. For example, I was taught how to wrap tefillin. If someone had told me that I would be wearing tefillin at seven in the morning for a prayer service, I would have said, "You're crazy." But, I did. On the first day, I felt like an alien. I didn't know "the how to" or the reasons "why." Then Rabbi William Lebeau, Vice Chancellor and Dean of the Rabbinical School, walked over to me and helped me wrap tefillin around my arm for the first time. I was physically wrapped, but what did this mean?

Rabbi Lebeau had a clear explanation. We wrap ourselves in God's good graces each and every day. Through this ritual, we are reminded that our bodies are strictly flesh. The richness of our blood pumps through our veins and pounds beneath the bindings. Our pulse humbles us. Our very existence relies on God's good graces. Tefillin binds us to God and to the Jewish people. By the second day of wrapping tefillin, I still felt strange, but I was warming up to the idea. Another vice chancellor of the seminary, Doctor Anne Lapidus Lerner, came to my aid. Now, two vice chancellors of the seminary helped me lay tefillin. That's a good way to begin.

While attending one particular morning service, I observed two attractive rabbinical students sitting right in front of me, preparing to daven (pray). As I watched this handsome couple wrap their tefillin, I experienced human magnetism that I have never witnessed before. The power that the male rabbinical student exuded in wrapping his arm, naturally, easily, and yet humbly will stay with me for the rest of my life. There is power, strength, and beauty in our religion that is not always spoken of—moments that impact our lives and cannot be easily described. I remain forever devoted to this ritual after witnessing this man and woman wrap tefillin on their arms—together, humbled before God.

Mr. Goodman

My ninety-year-old mentor, Mr. David Goodman, set the tone for my Jewish education. As one of the founding members of Temple Israel, he actively pursued the dream to move the congregation from a small house in the center of Ridgewood to its current location, a permanent building on Grove Street. I marveled at my Shabbat friend and looked forward to sitting with him every Saturday morning. Despite his hearing loss, David read Torah for the congregation well into his nineties, and inspired us all to continue our quest for Jewish knowledge and Hebrew literacy. While I sat beside him, I occasionally saw tears well up in his eyes. He was frustrated because his body would not cooperate. While his heart and soul cleaved to the synagogue, his body would not always oblige. One Shabbat morning, I witnessed the baby naming of his fourth generation. I will never forget his joy. It was a dream fulfilled for him to live long enough to see his great-grandchild named in the synagogue that he helped to create.

My last visit with Mr. Goodman was in his assisted living apartment. He had recently moved in and was happy give us a tour of the facility and his new living quarters. While on the tour, he pointed out his most precious possessions: a beautiful framed testimonial lithograph given to him by Temple Israel on his ninetieth birthday for a lifetime of service, his well-worn prayer book, and his tefillin that was frayed from years of devoted use. I was awed by his collection. Toward the end of his life, the items he treasured most were of religious value, ritual, and observance. Even after his death, his memory continues to be an inspiration to me. He was an example of spiritual wealth accumulated through Torah study.

I dreamt about Mr. Goodman, shortly after his death. I was contemplating a synagogue involvement decision. In the dream, he took me into a room that was filled with mouth-watering desserts, each one more appetizing, more scrumptious than the next. He said, "All these choices before you are excellent and each of them is the right one. Go ahead and pick, there are no wrong decisions. All your decisions will be good ones." I used this dream when honoring David's memory in a welcoming speech to new members of our congregation. I explained that there were many points of access to our community and many enticing options for involvement. All the choices are good ones.

Yizkor—To Remember

Yizkor is said in memory of a loved one. After my mother passed away, I knew that I was obligated to say Yizkor (memorial prayer), but I didn't understand why. However, one morning I woke up and saw that it was time to get up to recite Yizkor at synagogue. My mother, Lillian, had been deceased for eight years and my Aunt Mary had recently passed away. I didn't feel like getting out of bed so I rolled over and went back to sleep. As I dreamed, I pictured my mother and my aunt sitting on a pew, patiently awaiting my arrival. They were saving me a seat. When I woke up, I experienced a pang of intense longing, a deep desire for what I once had and was no longer available to me except during this memorial prayer service: their presence in my life. That morning, I realized the necessity of this vital connection. Yizkor is not only for the living to cope, but also for the dead to be remembered. We are united with our loved ones during these special prayers. After this dream, I rarely missed the chance to say these prayers for my parents. I knew it was an opportunity that I shouldn't waste.

Seven: Growing Up

To this day, I carry my dad's note that he had scribbled: "treat like a grown-up." How appropriate that I found this crumpled paper as I rummaged through his desk one bleak afternoon. I was weighed down by the intimidating responsibilities of attending to his estate. I struggled with adulthood as I faced my last parent's death.

On the nursing home floor, I sat by my father's bedside and waited. No words were exchanged and a peaceful silence engulfed the room. As the brilliant sun was setting, I felt a presence larger than both of us. We were not alone. I drifted off to sleep, seated upright in the hospital chair. As I dozed, my thoughts focused on the integrity that my dad, Myron Zimmerman, had brought into the world. I hoped that this fine quality would be transferred to me. I wanted to absorb his strengths, as his life was leaving mine. I sat there, just being there, with God and my dying father. I walked out of his room a better person than when I walked in.

During the course of my dad's critical illness, Americans experienced a catastrophic event. It shook us out of what we thought was our relatively secure existence. On September 11, 2001, terrorists flew two planes directly into the Twin Towers located in lower Manhattan. Millions of shocked people watched the buildings burn and collapse on television. First, Tower One fell and then Tower Two. Thousands lost their lives as the devastation unfolded. The horror was contrasted by a picture perfect, clear blue sky, now being filled with billowing smoke, fire, and ashes.

The night before the attack, Don placed a note on our bathroom mirror, "wear your best suit tomorrow," because he had a special meeting in midtown Manhattan. It was unusual that he had to commute to a midtown location and not to his downtown office. Most of the time he took the ferry that docked two blocks from the World Trade Center. That morning my friend Amy called and told me to turn the television on. I watched the inexplicable happen. Ten minutes later I jumped when Don called to say he was fine and that I shouldn't worry. He was going to find a way back to New Jersey. This was not an easy task because when he switched his suit the night before, he forgot to put his wallet in the coat pocket. That left him with no money or credit cards to pay for transportation home or for a hotel room. After the attack, he hiked from Thirty-Fourth Street over to the Citibank offices on Fifty-Third Street and Park where they quickly gave him a cash advance just as the building was being evacuated and locked down.

Don then spent several hours at the midtown offices of a client, Amerada Hess, because all mass transit, bridges, and tunnels were shut down. He decided the best way out of the city would be to hike up to the George Washington Bridge and walk across the Hudson River. While en route, he found out that the subway "A" train was running again. Compassionate New Yorkers helped him locate the easiest train connections, but when he arrived at the bridge, New Jersey–bound pedestrians were not permitted to walk across. Thousands of people were waiting in line for bus transportation. Don stood in this massive crowd when he heard a familiar voice calling out to him from the car lane: "Hurry up Donald, get in." Our rabbi, Noam Marans, had spotted Don in the mass of humanity. A good Samaritan from Ridgewood was giving the rabbi and his son a ride home and they had just enough room for one more passenger. I waited endlessly for the phone to ring and when it did, Rabbi Amy Roth (Noam's wife) notified me that Don was on his way home with Noam.

Rick Blood, a neighbor who lived down the street, died in the Twin Towers disaster. This wonderful, young father was taken from his beautiful wife and two young children for no apparent reason except that terrorists decided to make a statement. It was a tragic day. Many people live with this pain on a continual basis. May the memories of those lost that day live on, to recall the beauty and courage they instilled in us. May the survivors live on to honor all that is decent and ultimately good in the world.

The Jewish New Year of Rosh Hashanah followed in the wake of the Twin Towers devastation. I was assigned to chant the Second Day Haftarah, which took on a whole new meaning for me. The words spoken by the prophet Jeremiah were hauntingly relevant in the aftermath of the tragedy. These excerpts from the Haftarah addressed the vulnerable state of his nation and ours:

Thus saith the Lord:

The people that were left of the sword, Have found grace in the wilderness, Even Israel, when I go to cause him to rest. 'From afar the Lord appeared unto me.' Yea, I have loved thee with an everlasting love; Therefore with affection have I drawn thee. Again will I build thee, and thou shalt be built...
They shall come with weeping, And with supplications will I lead them; I will cause them to walk by rivers of waters, In a straight way wherein they shall not stumble... For I will turn their mourning into joy, And will comfort them, and make them rejoice from their sorrow. (Jeremiah 31:2–4, 31:9, 31:13; Hertz 1992)

The prophet's message of comfort and hope in the aftermath of the destruction of the Second Temple in Jerusalem was eerily appropriate when applied to the Twin Towers. His soothing words brought hope and asked us not to despair. Despite the onslaught of evil, God restores us to our faith. It is a message of faith for our time and for all time. God gives us hope to make the world a better place now and in the future regardless of the tragedies that we must endure along the way. The prophet's words of encouragement came at a time when people desperately needed them.

Could a rest for Israel be a worldwide sensitivity to what it means to be violated by terrorists? Suddenly, Americans experienced the horror that Israel and other nations experience daily. We became victims of despicable acts that threatened our sense of security. An overwhelming empathy seized our country for the victims of terrorism. A bomb's shattering effect became real to us and not simply headline news. Going shopping, going to work, or even walking the streets could turn into life threatening activities.

In the aftermath of the 9/11 attacks, there was an enormous groundswell of American patriotism. Up and down the East Coast, courageous acts made the headline news. Brave Americans lost their lives by valiantly attempting to retake their hijacked plane en route from Boston to Washington, D.C., with heroic efforts to save their fellow citizens on the ground below. Policemen, firemen, and other emergency workers also died heroically as they fought to save those caught in the devastation of the Twin Towers. The plane that crashed into the Pentagon caused more courageous men and women to plow into smoke and debris to aid survivors, even as they became victims themselves. The media focused on these "acts of loving-kindness." Positive energy fueled the headline news. People helped one another and came together as a community regardless of race or religion. The press indulged us with uplifting, good news. We watched and read about daring feats and enormous acts of compassion.

Media coverage often has a tendency to overlook the finer, more superior human qualities. It tends to concentrate on our unpleasant, lesser qualities. Most people are good, law-abiding citizens, but we are not always depicted that way. Many times we eye each other on the streets of America with suspicion. The vast majority of us are not bad at all. We actually do embody the noble and heroic public that the media portrayed us to be immediately after the terrorist attacks.

But bad news sells papers. Too often the media focuses on the lowest common denominator in life and makes the message seem universal in its coverage of an event. It would be to our benefit if the media highlighted the public's integrity and emphasized the good in humankind, not because it sells newspapers and not because it increases ratings, but because it is an important message of hope for our future.

A Role Reversal

Months after the attacks on US soil, Americans still traveled in fear. I thought about being blown up as I drove over the Delaware Memorial Bridge and through the Baltimore Harbor Tunnel to visit my dad. Since the attacks, it wasn't weird to wonder about your personal safety or what target would be next.

I saw my father's resilience throughout his illness. His triumphs were small compared to the nation's remarkable road to recovery. He desperately wanted to get back to a normal routine in his condominium but, unfortunately, that would never happen. He suffered from complications with diabetes, gout, and upper respiratory failure. I brought him diet root beer floats and I hand fed him because he could not feed himself. I wanted him to eat more, but he wouldn't. He was stubborn when he wanted to be. The nurse said to offer him anything he wanted to eat because he needed nourishment and not to worry about his sugar (the staff would regulate it). I was the parent now. He was the child, and I bore this responsibility heavily. I served him diet soda with a scoop of real vanilla ice cream (not sugar free). It didn't make a lot of sense, but neither did his impending death, or the recent deaths of so many innocent people.

I found it difficult to take the lead in this relationship, checking in with the doctors and nurses and making sure everything that could be done was being done. Without God's help, the task would have been overwhelming. My sister Bobbie and I split his care. She lived nearby and was able to visit him more often than I could. After an eight-hour day of teaching high-school Spanish, she sat in the hospital with him in the evening. Since I was living out of state, I stayed home during the day to speak to his doctors and oversee his financial matters. This job was more complicated than I originally thought. There were times when I was scared stiff of the new role I had to play in his life.

Fortunately, my sister and I had additional family support close by. Our older cousin, Martin, lived right around the corner from the hospital in Bethesda, Maryland, and he helped us out whenever he could. My dad's brother, Alan, residing in Washington, D.C., saw my father every week and fed him lunch. I remember one lonely Shabbat afternoon. I was overly anxious about my dad's care when our cousins, the Wasco family, suddenly walked in. Jeri, Barry, Noah, and Renee brightened up my life that day. The family support systems were readily available, and my sister and I kept tapping into them.

One morning, my dad confided to me over the phone, "I didn't have a good night last night." I asked why. He replied, "A nurse left me in my wheelchair facing the wall for hours until she came back to get me ready for bed." I hated the idea of him alone, vulnerable, and sitting there facing the wall. After that, we hired an extra nurse on the weekends to stay beside him. We couldn't bear the thought of him being so helpless. It was too much for us to think about.

My visits to my father were surprisingly rewarding. Despite the pain of the impending loss, the process of letting go was natural and necessary. As he began to leave this world, I grew stronger, more secure, and aware of a greater force in our lives. I don't want to say this was easy, but God's direction made it bearable. It was not beyond my capacity to cope; I managed to get through it.

While my dad was dying, we had a wonderful simcha (joyous occasion) to lift my spirits. When I was not taking care of my father's needs, I planned my youngest daughter's Bat Mitzvah. Tiffany and I shopped for her dress, picked out invitations, and shared enjoyable activities in preparation for her special day. We practiced her haftarah (the prophet's words) together, as a peaceful reprieve. It was this simcha that kept me emotionally balanced. I knew I was losing my father, but so much of life was still going on around me. How can your heart soar when it is breaking in two? Triumphs are won on a daily basis.

I traveled to Virginia to see my dad when telephone calls just weren't enough. On one visit I walked into his room and saw his face light up with a big smile when I entered. I mean not just a little, his face really lit up, like I was the only person on earth. It's a radiance that comes to a parent's face for their child. I observed it once when my cousin Lois arrived to see her mom, my Aunt Rose. The expression is a mixture of happiness, pride, and pure joy. I am grateful that I was able to witness my father's parental glow, appreciate it, and clearly remember it. One afternoon, while I sat by his bedside, my dad woke up and said, "Are you still here?" I guess he thought that I had left. He was so pleased to see me. I received that special gift of recognition all over again.

I joined my father in the dining hall whenever I could because it was his only social outlet. He was seated with three elderly ladies, one of whom became a special person to us. Sally was dying of cancer, but despite her physical adversity she was optimistic and charming. She was blessed with a graceful dignity, and I took great comfort in her spirit. Each day Sally made our difficult situation more bearable.

My father and I were fortunate to say, "I love you" every day of his illness. In addition, the remarkable nurses became close to our family. One very sympathetic nurse, Nellie, took me aside and said, "When he dies, you must remember to go on with your life and not be too upset because you and your sister, Bobbie, have been good daughters. Your relationship is such that he should depart from you in peace. Also, Myron has never lost his sense of humor or his humanity. He will die with dignity and not everyone can do that."

A Bat Mitzvah Reprieve

Tiffany's Bat Mitzvah was a welcome oasis from grief. I spent a considerable amount of time studying the Torah parashah (portion from the Old Testament) that I would chant the morning of her special day. The studying helped me get through the last two months of my father's illness. The parashah that I read was as follows:

> So Jacob named the place Peniel, meaning, "I have seen a divine being face to face, yet my life has been preserved." The sun rose upon him as he passed Penuel, limping on his hip. That is why the children of Israel to this day do not eat the thigh muscle that is on the socket of the hip, since Jacob's hip socket was wrenched at the thigh muscle. Looking up, Jacob saw Esau coming, accompanied by four hundred men. He divided the children among Leah, Rachel, and the two maids, putting the maids and their children first, Leah and her children next, and Rachel and Joseph last. He himself went on ahead and bowed low to the ground seven times until he was near his brother. Esau ran to greet him. He embraced him and, falling on his neck, he kissed him; and they wept. Looking about, he saw the women and the children. "Who," he asked, "are these with you?" He answered, "The children with whom God has favored your servant." (Genesis 32:31–33, 33:1–5; Rabbinical 1999)

My interpretation is that Jacob wrestled with an angel all night as he struggled with his own humanity. He grappled with his inability to be a perfect man with the voice of God in his head—how can I be so imperfect and yet have the ability to hear the Almighty? What makes me so special that I can win God's favor? The next day, Jacob must face a frightening situation with his twin brother. Jacob does not know how Esau, who he wronged by stealing his birthright, will respond.

Jacob's struggles are poignantly human. His ability to communicate with God is not so unique because his father Isaac, his mother, Rebecca, and his grandparents Abraham and Sarah, had the ability to converse with God. Jacob experiences God face to face and can no longer run from his problems. As a child, Jacob turned away but now, as an adult, he faces his destiny. He ultimately has no choice because he cannot hide from either God or himself.

Jacob meets Esau and the encounter goes much better than he expected. Jacob moved his most precious family members to the back of the group. Why? He realizes, sadly, that if he were to be attacked by Esau, he could better protect those closest to him. But instead of a brutal confrontation, Esau embraces Jacob and they both cry. When Esau inquires about the people he has brought with him, Jacob gives credit to God for giving him his children. The change in Jacob is immediate. He is now a humble servant of the Lord.

When I walked away from this Torah reading at Tiffany's Bat Mitzvah, I gained a much-needed focus. I had to find the courage to face my flaws, regardless of how frightened I was at the impending death of my father. As I neared the loss of my last surviving parent, I felt a closer, more adult relationship with God. I came to accept my new place in life. In the parashah, Jacob said these are the children that God has blessed me with. I was able to say the same because my three children read Torah with me that day.

Saying Goodbye

My joy was tempered by the fact that I would see my dad only one more time. Two weeks after the Bat Mitzvah, I was mentally preparing myself for the inevitable outcome. He was not going to recover. He wasn't going to go back to his condominium and resume a normal life. His quality of life had completely degenerated. He could not feed himself, walk, or get out of bed. He wasn't swallowing his food and he refused a feeding tube. He was aspirating, which would eventually lead to pneumonia because of fluid backup in his lungs. He wore a diaper. He was dependent on everyone, but no one could help him get better. He was dying and this time there would be no reprieve.

When his pain became excruciating and painkillers were necessary, my father never complained. Fortunately, the pain did not last more than a day before the hospice nurse arrived with morphine. I don't know how he went day by day with his body falling apart, but he did. He showed great strength of human spirit and despite his ordeal, he held onto his dignity. But he did not talk, nor did he want to talk, about death or his dying.

During one of my last visits, I met his psychiatrist, Doctor Dean Storer. The doctor and I had spoken on the phone many times over the last two years and I was pleased to finally meet him. He offered me sound advice on how to proceed, since I was so uncertain as to how to say goodbye. I asked him if I should discuss dying with my dad. Doctor Storer said only if he wants to discuss this with you. Otherwise, enjoy the time you have left together. That evening I wheeled my dad up to the third floor of his retirement home during a lively holiday party. I decided a festive atmosphere wouldn't hurt for a little while and he might even see some old friends.

I pushed his wheelchair throughout the partygoers and everyone said, "Hello, Myron. It's so nice to see you, we've missed you." My father had a huge smile on his face and was delighted to see them. It is interesting that, except for maybe one person, no one came to the nursing home floor to visit my dad. From their expressions, I think my dad's condition hit too close to home and seeing him incapacitated made them very uncomfortable. At that point, my father certainly did not look the picture of health, but he had a nice time and for a few brief moments, he enjoyed the holiday festivities in the gaily-decorated lounge. After wheeling him around this party atmosphere for an hour, he said, "I've had enough," so I brought him back upstairs to the nursing home floor. Later that night, he said to me, "It was great of you to throw that party for me today. You are a real sweetheart!"

The final day of my visit, I sat quietly with my father. During his nap, I stopped in to see Sally, the wonderful lady who often ate with us in the dining hall. She was pleased to see me. Throughout the course of our conversation, she questioned why God was keeping her on earth, knowing that she would die soon. Sally was concerned about money because the Jefferson (retirement home) was expensive, and she also worried that her lovely daughter devoted too much time visiting her. I reassured her that she shouldn't worry about the money at this point. Her daughter loved her and gladly spent this time with her. As I was soothing Sally, the mitzvah (good deed) came right back to me.

Sally began describing me. At first, I assumed she had been talking to my dad about me, but I realized quickly that she was saying things that had no relation to my dad (plus he was not a particularly emotive person). She spoke from my mother's perspective, but my mom had been deceased for over nine years. Sally commented that I looked like my mother only with blond hair. She said, "Your mom is so proud of you...she is 'bragalicious' about you in heaven." It was such an unusual term, bragalicious, that I couldn't forget it. Sally painted a picture of my mother joyously watching over me. I thanked Sally for her caring words because she had provided me with remarkable support when I most needed it. I replied, "Maybe God has kept you on earth for this very moment to assist someone like me who desperately needs your comfort."

I knew it was the last time I would see my dad, but now I understood that my mother was up in heaven watching and waiting for him to join her. I was completely comforted by this thought. I believed that Sally's support came from a greater source, as she was able to bridge life and death (heaven and earth) being so close to death herself. Sally died a week later, on Christmas, five days after my father.

As the last hour of my scheduled visit with my dad approached, I remained with him and dozed off, as he slept. We were sitting side by side. He was propped up in the bed and I was next to him seated upright in a hospital chair. For a few moments, we both remained in a peaceful sleep. I'm not sure exactly what occurred, but I do know that something did. It was more a feeling than anything else, as if his fine attributes were being imprinted on me. All the positive memories came up from our last five months together including my increased ability to take care of his financial and medical needs, his dignity and strength throughout his illness, and his optimism and good nature throughout his ordeal. He continually let me know how much he loved me without ever discussing his impending death. I awoke with these good feelings, knowing that this exchange somehow involved God.

I looked out into the setting sun and saw a radiant, blue sky streaked with strands of white clouds. I knew that we were not alone in the room. I had a bright future to look forward to with my husband and children. My father would be relieved of his physical pain and be reunited with my mother. The tears fell as I said good-bye that late, sunny afternoon. I knew that I wouldn't see him again. I told him that I loved him, and he said that he loved me. He saw my tears and said, "You have tears of joy." I fought them back because in so many ways, he was right, they were tears of joy, not sorrow. His life ebbed away as mine continued to flow.

I returned home, waiting for the inevitable, but not wanting it to occur. It was a relief to continually speak to him every day and tell him that I loved him. The last week before he died, it became increasingly more difficult to reach him. Occasionally, he was not able to pick up the telephone or even hear it ring. One evening, after not getting in touch with him for the second time in a row, I decided that—this is the end. I must get ready to lose him now. On that same night, Nellie, our good friend and special nurse, went out of her way to go to my father's phone and pick it up for him. I was able to tell him that I loved him very much. He got out the words, "I love you too," and then the rest was garbled. That was the last time I spoke to him. He died the next morning on December 20, 2001.

We only wanted our immediate family at the funeral. My cousins, Lois Stark and Gary Lessen, came on their way to Myrtle Beach, South Carolina. I was so happy to see them. What good cousins and friends they are to us. When the dirt went over my dad's coffin I felt like I couldn't breathe, but my daughter Tammie stood next to me rubbing my back while Zachary chanted the prayers in Hebrew, soothing my soul. I knew I would get through this. I was annoyed with Donald about something or other, but later, as we stood over my father's grave, his comments made me break a smile. It was not unusual for Donald to get me to laugh through difficult times. He admitted, "I am all you have now. I guess you are stuck with me." He was half joking and half serious. I knew everything would be fine as I laughed through my tears.

Now that my Mom and Dad rested peacefully in their graves, it was time for me to take care of my family. I knew that I had to turn away from their cemetery plots and move on. After the funeral, we came back to the house to eat a quiet Shabbat dinner together. We needed Shabbat to help make our family whole again.

A little background on family dynamics is necessary here. The night my dad died, Tammie went jogging with Zachary. She turned her ankle and I went "bananas" about how stupid it was that they went jogging the night of my father's funeral. I had to drive Tammie to the emergency room because her ankle ballooned up very badly. I approached the nurse at the emergency station and said, "I'm having a rough day. I just buried my dad and I think my daughter's ankle is broken." I was exhausted, and yet I was being a mom on the day I buried my dad. Fortunately, it was a sprain and they gave her a soft cast to wear. Good thing they told us it would turn various shades of purple and not to be concerned. The next day, every color of the rainbow appeared on that ankle.

We had a memorial service for my dad at our synagogue. I called several friends and the word quickly spread. Over sixty people attended. Before the service began, I had a brief conversation with Rabbi Gil Steinlauf who kindly informed me that a Jewish conversion class would be starting right away. He thought the timing might be right for Don to participate. I suggested that he ask Don directly. Rabbi Steinlauf left the room, came back, and said he had just spoken to Don. Don said he was not ready to convert, but that he would be interested in taking the class. You can only imagine how pleased I was to hear this right before my father's memorial service. It was exactly what I needed to hear.

I was grateful for everyone who attended the memorial service on such short notice. I wanted to do justice to my dad's memory and this is what came out.

> My father taught me so much in these past few months. I had to 'step up to the plate' and handle jobs for him that I did not want to do. I know he saw me change and although he was a man of very few words, he told me that he loved me and was proud of me. At the same time, I was proud of him too. He never acted poorly around me even when his condition worsened, and he knew the end was coming. He was stoic and a gentleman to the end. Although quite uncomfortable, he sat there, day after day and did not allow it to sway his natural optimism. My father gave me the courage to do what I had to do for him, and I gave him strength with my visits. I showed him I was flourishing even as he was dying. What better gift to give a parent in the end: your love, and yet your full independence.

Dreams to Remember

I had unusual dreams about my dad after he passed away. One night, as I slept, I longed to speak with him. I still worried about him. In my dream, I looked down to find a walkie-talkie in my hand, and I called for him. I heard back in a clear voice. "Myron Zimmerman here!" I was shocked because it was his voice. I didn't know how to respond, so I said, "How are you?" He replied, "I'm great!" I hadn't heard him sound so good since before his illness. The dream was extremely vivid and I was comforted by it.

Another dream happened thirty days into my mourning period. I was sitting on a bench with my sister, Bobbie, and our father was seated lower on the bench to my right. All of a sudden our deceased Aunt Mary showed up! She looked beautiful and radiantly happy. She was young, younger than I had ever imagined her to be. Aunt Mary spoke kindly to my father, encouraging him to come along with her. She was saying wonderful things to him about his life and reassuring him that everything would be all right. She was coaxing him to move on and to take the next step.

My aunt and dad did not have this loving relationship on earth. I was surprised when I heard her tone and how compassionately she spoke to him. After the dream, I realized it was the final day of shloshim, the immediate thirty-day mourning period after my father's death. Apparently, my dad was moving to his soul's resting place and my aunt was showing him the way. I was grateful for this dream. It brought me peace of mind.

After my father died, I sometimes felt him around me, especially when I sat down to pay the rest of his bills and resolve his credit card debt. He had two outstanding credit card bills when he died and I knew that they would have bothered him. For the first thirty days after his death, his presence was around encouraging me to finish what I had to accomplish. There was a real urgency to finish what he wanted me to do, as if his final resting place depended on it. How do I know this? I just felt it. I felt him nearby. I felt the relief once the job was done. It was visceral, nothing you could put your finger on, and yet, I knew it to be true.

These dreams and memories of my dad soothed me at a time when I missed him. I missed our phone conversations. I missed him being there. I missed being his daughter. I missed having parents and I missed being a child. I was no longer a daughter. My husband could not be my parent because he was my spouse. I had to look at myself and realize that this is it. I was the responsible one. Now that I was parentless, a bond was broken and a new stage in my life had begun.

Eight: Let's Move to Hawaii

Don lost his job. Many of his colleagues, successful middle managers who had worked on Wall Street for more than twenty-five years, were fired in the aftermath of September 11. Don had worked hard all those years to preserve our New Jersey lifestyle, pay for colleges, and save for retirement. He left the house at seven in the morning and did not arrive home until late at night. This exhausting routine appeared to be endless. His job had become a constant grind. He no longer enjoyed investment banking or most of the people he was working with.

He spent the entire day Saturday sleeping and resting so by Sunday, he was close to normal, but there wasn't much time left for the family. On Wall Street, there were many good years and a few depressingly bad ones. Don felt the pressure of continuing the family's lifestyle in an upper middle class neighborhood. We did not live extravagantly, but it was expensive to live in Bergen County, New Jersey. From the start of our family, we had agreed that one parent would stay home. I won.

After Don lost his job, he had a balanced perspective on the situation. Friends in town kept him busy with tennis, golf, poker, band practice, and sushi lunches. He was getting his life back again. We had already planned and paid for a trip to Hawaii, so we decided to go anyway. This vacation would accelerate a pivotal decision in our lives.

In December of 2001 after Tiffany's Bat Mitzvah and my dad's death, we flew from Newark, New Jersey, on a bitterly cold morning, into a warm, balmy evening in Honolulu. After a couple of days on Oahu, Don turned to me and said, "I want to live here." I replied, "Are you crazy? It's too far away, we don't know anyone here, we have a beautiful home, a community in Ridgewood, and our extended family lives on the East Coast." I hoped his dream would disappear. A few hours later, I took the children out to dinner in Waikiki, but he wouldn't budge. He was upset with my indifference to Hawaii, and for a split second, despite my anger with him, I realized that I missed him. Being together as a family meant everything to me. As crazy as it sounds, I turned to Tiffany and blurted out, "If Dad needs us to live here, I'll move because I want to be with your father." I still didn't think we would actually do it.

We returned from Hawaii and upon arrival I felt like a ton of bricks hit me. My dad was gone and we were back in freezing cold New Jersey. It took two weeks for us to recover from jet lag. I don't remember ever sleeping so much before. So where do we go from here? Don was out of work and home for the first time in twenty-five years. How did I ever adjust to his long hours on the job when having him around now was so much better? He joined an "out placement" program and I considered taking a full time job. Don needed a break from commuting into New York City, and I thought I might try going back to work. Change was in the air. We had to adapt and resolve this together. If I became the breadwinner after all these years of staying home with the children, we wouldn't make enough money to maintain our current lifestyle, pay for colleges, and eventually retire.

A week after returning home from Hawaii, Don, Tammie, and I were sitting around the Friday night dinner table discussing our future. Don and Tammie began a serious conversation about permanently moving to Oahu. Tammie was a sophomore at Ridgewood High School and she decided we should move immediately. Don was not far behind her. We all agreed that if we moved, it would take us a while to pull up stakes and sell our home. A minimum of a year would be necessary to unwind our lives in Ridgewood.

The more they talked about moving, the more uncomfortable I felt. I was not prepared to leave my extended family on the East Coast. During this discussion, I angrily left the dinner table, marched up to my room, and slammed the door. It was a disruptive conversation on Shabbat. I felt terrible. Could a move be possible? Why Hawaii? Certainly, there were many other beautiful places to relocate. Don had lived with his family on Oahu when his father, a career army officer, was stationed there. Don spent a good part of his teenage years on the island with his parents and brother, Jesse. Evidently, Don never forgot his love for Hawaii or his desire to eventually return.

I vividly remembered our first family Hawaiian vacation in 1998 when he escorted us down memory lane. I immediately noticed how comfortable he was driving around the island. As we toured Oahu, he took us to some of his favorite spots. We explored the places where he had lived—Fort Shafter, Schofield Barracks, and Queen Emma Gardens. As we drove around his middle school and high school, he described his experiences of being a white minority student in the 1960s. During these expeditions, Zachary, Tammie, and Tiffany sat in the back of the rental car giggling and teasing each other. Occasionally a head would pop up from the backseat when we pointed out an interesting sight.

Our stops included the famous Matsumoto Shave Ice store in Haleiwa and beaches on the North Shore. Don showed us prime spots where he had surfed for hours after school with his high school buddies. Sometimes during our beach breaks, he stood captivated watching the waves, transfixed on the shore. He wouldn't hear me when I called out to him. We drove along the roadside beaches and stopped to snorkel our way around coral reefs. Beach hopping provided a complete sense of freedom that I had never experienced before. As our vacation days progressed,

I realized something was a lot different about this man I married when we were in Hawaii.

The Big Island was our next adventure. This impressive island alternates between a combination of volcanic, moon-like terrain and lush rain forests. In Hilo, we splurged on a helicopter ride over an active volcano. It was expensive, but worth it. I remember hovering over an oozing mass of bubbling fire and gas with molten pockets of lava spurting up toward us. We gazed below in disbelief with a mixture of curiosity and awe.

We continued onto Maui where we explored the famous whaling port of Lahaina. It was there that we saw an enormous banyan tree that spread over an entire block, the largest tree of its kind in the islands. We had made hotel reservations, but the accommodations were wrong when we arrived. This worked out to our advantage when we were placed in a glorious, private, two-bedroom, ground level condominium in the middle of an exotic garden by the beach. We went to our first luau as the sun was setting over the ocean and we watched the fire dancer in utter amazement as he juggled flaming wands around in the air. After two days on Maui and realizing it wasn't enough, we said we would come back another time for more. Little did I realize, how soon or how much more.

We both loved Hawaii. It was the obvious choice for us to start over, yet after all of these years, how could we do it? I spent tons of time thinking about all the pros and cons of this type of move. And every Shabbat I asked God, "Is this what you want of me?" And every week during this quiet time, I found my answer. Don spent twenty-five years providing for us. Wasn't it his turn to live in a stress-free environment with the opportunity to remake his life? In New Jersey, he took the enjoyment when he could, on the weekends and family vacations, or playing tennis, softball, and poker with his friends. But Hawaii somehow made him come alive again as we snorkeled, surfed, and hiked around the island.

On the other hand, my life for the last twenty-five years had been very rewarding. I stayed home to be a full-time parent and volunteered extensively in our congregation. My days consisted of leisurely outings with the children and carpooling to their after school activities. I particularly looked forward to family holidays and gatherings in our home because we were centrally located between the cousins. Living this kind of life was all I ever wanted. The joke of Don's tennis group was that they each wanted to come back in their next life as a Ridgewood housewife.

Don trudged into the city every weekday. He worked extremely long hours and looked lousy. Our lives were out of balance. When I took a moment to stop enjoying myself and look at him, I would say, "I suppose it isn't fair for us to have it so good while you're the mule." He replied, "If you and the children are happy that makes me happy." We continued to live this out-of-kilter lifestyle until he lost his job.

More questions about moving to Hawaii continued to plague me. Could I say good-bye to my friends and leave behind our family on the East Coast? What about the Jewish community that we loved in Ridgewood? Could I leave our beautiful house of eighteen years? What about our furniture that had taken us so much time and effort to accumulate? We worked on the house on weekends or weeknights when Don was done with work—and tired. Although some of our closest friends and neighbors had moved away years ago, I was determined to "stay put" no matter what. I liked where we were and the children were happy. We watched the neighborhood change around us, but we remained close to our previous neighbors and made friends with the new ones.

I didn't want to leave our garden and koi pond. When I mentioned the garden to Tammie she responded, "Come on Mom, all of Hawaii is a garden. Look at what you are gaining, not losing." Her comment sunk in. Our decision to move was not quick or easy. Yet, despite our good life in New Jersey, Hawaii seemed to be a win-win situation for all of us.

Many scenarios popped into my head during our decision-making. Don would exercise and get his weight down. He would be happier and certainly healthier. He would be home for meals during the week and have more time for his teenage daughters, quality time that they all needed. Don would sit at the head of the table and join us at our Friday night dinners. Shabbat afternoons would be spent together at the beach after we attended services. When Zachary came home to Hawaii from college, he would go surfing with his dad. Zachary had the least amount of quality time with his father while growing up and this would give them a chance to bond. A lot of positive thoughts jumped into my head as I thought about this move.

It was finally decided that Tammie and Don would take an extended trip to Hawaii and do some research firsthand. They went the summer of 2002 while the high schools were in session. Tammie would be a senior and Tiffany would be an incoming freshman at Kalaheo High School. An energetic real estate agent from Coldwell Banker showed them around the housing market on the windward side of the island. As I helped plan their itinerary, I didn't realize that this trip would create such a solid foundation for our first year of island living.

Throughout our Hawaii deliberations, I was still in mourning for my father. What does that mean in Jewish law? I was not permitted to go to movies, attend parties or celebrations for eleven months after his death. As incredibly active as I had been, I adjusted to the idea. I used this opportunity to regroup and pay attention to my family. Loads of paperwork surrounded me while I organized my father's affairs. I considered myself an extrovert, but now I was forced to settle down and accomplish what I needed to do. This introspective period helped me get comfortable with our decision to move.

I worked hard to make this move happen. I couldn't sit around and expect Don to do all the research on a life-changing decision of this magnitude. The preparation for the move was exhilarating and scary at the same time. When I called the Department of Education in Hawaii, friendly people answered the telephone instead of electronic voice prompts. I talked to grade administrators and nurses. Hawaii residents had all the time in the world for me as they patiently listened and responded to my endless questions. Surprisingly, they never ended the conversation first.

I called the University of Hawaii for Tammie and set up a tour of the facilities and campus. The advantage was that East Coast time is several hours ahead of Hawaiian time. When I spoke to someone interesting I reported back to Don, and together we poured over the incoming information. I met Lisa for lunch, our wonderful "pro Hawaii" friend. Her family had previously lived on Oahu for many years. Lisa identified attractive neighborhoods while offering us a wealth of knowledge and a list of her friends to contact.

Hawaii was my project. Many afternoons, I sat in my New Jersey garden and called Oahu. Sure, I was nervous. I did not always want to make the call, but I was happy after I did it. Like doing my volunteer work for the congregation, I was elated afterward. Now, I was doing something extremely important for my family. I spoke to Rabbi Avi Magid and Cantor Ken Aronowitz at the Reformed synagogue, Temple Emanu-El. I called the Conservative synagogue, Congregation Sof Ma'arav, and spoke to Bernice Littman (the president) and her husband Robert (the treasurer). I spoke to the Chabad Rabbi, Rabbi Itchel Krasnjansky. As my research continued and I accumulated more and more information, I became enamored of the Jewish community in Hawaii. Once I realized that we could keep a kosher home in Hawaii, it was a done deal.

Nine: A Conversion

Beginnings are the hardest. Everyone has the same problem, but once you get started, everything falls into place. I can think of many examples: paying bills, losing weight, doing exercise programs, looking for a job, painting a picture, or writing a book. Starting is the most difficult task of all. This is true of most activities that involve transition. Many times the change is good and inevitable. Both courage and discipline are necessary to do it. Yet sometimes we act like children instead of adults. We would rather have everything come to us easily rather than changing our comfortable ways. It is simpler and less scary to settle on a familiar route even if it makes us miserable.

I leaned over our dining room table in New Jersey, holding my head in my hands, trying to deal with my father's death and his financial matters. I was completely overwhelmed by change. If you had said that I would be relocating to Hawaii and leaving a community that I worked so hard to create, I would have replied, "You're crazy! I love living in Ridgewood." Of course, I hadn't faced twelve to fourteen-hour days in a difficult job dealing with the constant threat of layoffs like my husband did. The move would restore our family's equilibrium.

When we told our friends that we would be moving to Hawaii, there was a steady murmur of "You've got to be kidding." Most of them were not of retirement age and they were staying put for a while. Going to live in Hawaii was like going to live on the moon—unthinkable.

Don converted to Judaism after twenty-five years of marriage. This change occurred during our New Jersey to Hawaii transition. Rabbi Batya Steinlauf, our rabbi's wife, began a conversion class in February of 2002, two months after my Dad died, and a few months after Don lost his job. I was shocked to hear that the class was for couples only. I hoped Don would take the class alone because I was afraid to do this with him. What if I said something wrong and he decided not to convert? At this point, it was extremely important for me to have the conversion take place and I didn't want my feelings to jeopardize his decision.

Despite years of us both being active in synagogue life, the conversion class filled gaps in our Jewish education. We studied again, together. Our weekly meetings with other couples seeking a new religious path were friendly and encouraging. Conversations thrived amid the group's diverse backgrounds. Together we explored the fundamentals of Judaism and applied them to each of us. Rabbi Batya Steinlauf taught us with a wealth of knowledge, patience, and kindness. Her only fee was the cost of the babysitter. When childcare was not available, she continued the classes in her living room, often cuddling a child on her lap.

Since Donald was already circumcised, the final stage of his conversion was a symbolic circumcision, with a mohel drawing a tiny drop of blood (hatafat dam brit). Don said it didn't hurt. I was incredibly nervous, but as usual it was fine. The next morning he was interviewed by the beit din, a rabbinic court consisting of three rabbis. They asked him questions to judge the validity of his conversion. The final step was an immersion and purification in the ritual bath, the mikvah. Here is Don's conversion statement:

> I feel that I am Jewish. I head a Jewish household. My children, my wife, and I are all practicing Jews. We celebrate Shabbat and the festivals, we keep kosher, we attend

synagogue, we support Israel, and we continue to evolve in our Jewish lifestyle.

I am converting so that I can more fully participate in Jewish life. I would like to receive aliyot, lead prayer services, study Torah, and even wear tefillin. I also want to be buried with my wife.

My family has traveled to Jerusalem. My son and I hiked down Masada after Shabbat services there. We also participated in Friday night services at the Kotel. My friends are mostly Jews. As Ruth said: 'Your God is my God, your people are my people.'

I chose the Hebrew names of Micah and Noah. Micah's summary of Jewish obligation resonates with me: do justice, love goodness, and walk humbly with God. Micah's name will remind me to balance justice with compassion and not judge too harshly. Noah humbly helped God save the world. His name and Hawaii's rainbows will remind me of God's mercy and his compassion for all people. My family is moving to Hawaii next summer and we expect to join Congregation Sof Ma'arav on the island of Oahu.

In an interview by the local paper, Don said this about his conversion (*Ridgewood News—Gloria Geannette*, 4/18/03):

Except for certain questions of faith, our religions were grounded in the same traditions, so it was not too difficult for me to make the change. At first I took part mostly in the Temple's social activities, but gradually I became more attracted to the spiritual aspects as well. I wanted to participate more and more in the synagogue. My goal was to be able to read from the Torah someday.

Rabbi Gil Steinlauf who converted Donald was quoted from the *Jewish Standard* ("*Turning Point*," by Joanne Palmer, 5/2/03):

It is very important to us that there are a number of intermarried families in our community. We want them to feel welcome, to feel that they have a place here. Everyone is on his or her own path; everyone goes in his or her own way. We are in the business of offering opportunities for learning and experiencing what Judaism is and what it means in their lives. Donald's experience is a celebration of that process. He's always found that he has a place in our synagogue, and now he's at a place where it feels right for him to adopt a Jewish identity.

The day that Donald converted was both exceptional and ordinary. Change is sometimes matter of fact and causes nothing more than a brief blip in our hectic schedules. Other times, change is so dramatic and unexpected that we halt completely. Don's conversion was a natural culmination to his evolving Jewish faith. A Shabbat does not go by without me marveling at his transformation. I sit in synagogue and try to remember the many times when I sat alone, without him. I am awed by the difference his conversion has made in our lives. One ordinary day, a regular kind of day, with no more than a brief ceremony along the way, changed our lives forever.

Ten: The Mikvah

Now that I had a Jewish husband, I felt obligated to fulfill the laws of family purity, which meant dipping into the water of a ritual bath on a monthly basis to purify myself. The mikvah represents change, transforming a person into more than they could ever hope to be. The first time I went to the mikvah was with a good friend, Barbara. She held my hand all the way, as she ran out to do this good deed (leaving four children at home to do homework was not easy for her). One blustery, cold evening, we entered the mikvah building together, side-by-side.

At the mikvah, I took a final shower and prepared myself for immersion in the water. When I submerged slowly, something unusual happened. As I stretched out face down in the water, my body kept floating up to the surface. I could not stay down. It was startling, and then I understood why. My life was buoyant. God held me up. Why should I fret about everything all the time, the move, the children, and Don? I wasn't going to sink. Belief would create lightness in my life. I tried to remember these positive feelings throughout the month, but there were times when I forgot. I worried, but I found myself moving closer to accepting and responding to God's direction in my life. The mikvah became a critical link to my spiritual development.

I was extremely nervous about using it for the first time. What if I am not thoroughly clean? Will I damage the water for the next person? Barbara assured me that this is not so. Will I ever be clean enough to appear before God? Despite all my insecurities, the next time I went to the mikvah, I went alone. The attendant was patiently reassuring and she seemed to understand my concerns.

A mikvah attendant takes on the responsibility for your proper immersion. These attendants, often complete strangers, spare a few moments to care about your spiritual well being and attend to your physical needs. I found this meticulous care mystifying. During one visit, the attendant noticed that I had a little nail polish left on my toes. She went to the back room, returned with nail polish remover, bent down, and cleaned off my toes. I was preparing to enter the water and someone I had never met before took the time to perfect me. In this one instance, I understood the mitzvah of kindness to a stranger. This simple act of compassion generated enormous empathy.

Each immersion taught me something new. Sometimes the learning occurred during preparation, and other times, it was while I was deep in the water. The attendant watches you dip under the water two or three times, depending on your tradition. You must be completely covered by water, without touching the bottom or the sides of the pool. When you do it right, the attendant says, "Kosher."

One time I touched the wall of the mikvah. The attendant said, "You must do it again. You did not do it right." At that point in my life, I had been trying to do too much. Don was flying back and forth to Hawaii and I was handling the bulk of the "moving" preparations. Needless to say, I was stressed. With the attendant's direction, I realized that I was relying too much on myself. Certainly others were out there to lend me a hand. I needed to ask for help. I looked forward to the insight gained from these monthly visits.

Another evening, I entered the mikvah seeking guidance. It was a pivotal time in my life. I was anxious about the sale of the New Jersey house and our impending move to Hawaii. I felt overwhelmed as I submerged. I was scared and worried. After a few minutes alone with God, I walked out of the water and felt chemically rearranged, organically renewed, and invigorated once again. I was empowered and ready to face the challenges that just moments ago I thought were way over my head. Without this ritual, the change would have been too strenuous, like carrying bricks on my back. It was the monthly physical reminder of God's hand in my life that revitalized my body and soul. No other ritual in Judaism could comfort me in the same manner.

A ritual involving water and immersion makes sense. Every month a married woman is required to immerse herself in the mikvah, to be cleansed. Every month a potential life has formed in her body. When she loses that life in the form of blood, she must wait seven days and cleanse herself in the mikvah. This allows her to resume relations with her husband.

The Miracle of the Mikvah

The miracle of the mikvah can be found in the preparation, as well as the immersion. How many times in the month do we take the time to observe our glorious bodies? We go for a manicure or pedicure, if we are fortunate. We walk away feeling radiant. But how many times do we take the opportunity to see how wonderful we really are? We have the ability to perceive our beauty like no other animal does.

Observing the beautiful creatures that God created, our bodies are our delight. Heavy or thin, tall or short, they are ours. Once a month, we prepare our bodies and our souls. Cleansing our bodies from top to bottom, removing dead skin, cleaning our fingernails, and flossing our teeth.

We pull a comb slowly through our hair and contemplate who we are and why we are here. We know in preparation for the ritual immersion that we will have a special time with God. It will be a personal moment of prayer and reflection, and a chance for monthly introspection. We go into the water by ourselves; we come out certain that we are renewed by faith. We are stronger, and even more beautiful than we were going in, because through this ritual, we are reminded of the importance of our lives.

Good relationships/bad relationships, it doesn't really matter, the water brings us closer to our maternal origins. We think of our mothers in the velvety warmth of the waters surrounding us. We were cuddled and comforted in their warm embrace. Every month, as we purge ourselves from the loss of life inside us, we remember who gave us life. As mature adults, we immerse in the water and instinctively remember our beginning. We come back to the water to re-experience the love, the peace, and the innocence of a baby in the womb. At the moment of immersion, we feel rejuvenated. We emerge purified with renewed security, hope, and confidence. As adults, with families of our own, we have a million tasks to fulfill, and yet we are commanded to take the time to enter the waters. We may no longer physically have our mothers, but we understand the true delight of being eternally embraced.

Eleven: Under the Huppah

"Can we get married again?" I asked Evan Dobkins, the president of Temple Israel. Change is good, but remarrying the same man could be even better. We wanted a religious ceremony to sanctify our relationship after Don's conversion with a signed ketubah (Jewish wedding contract). Originally, we contemplated a quick wedding in the rabbi's office before our departure to Hawaii. Since we were going to be honored at a testimonial dinner fundraiser for the synagogue, our wedding ceremony would be icing on the cake. We would get married under a huppah (wedding canopy) with our son and two daughters as attendants, among a community that we loved. It doesn't get better than that. I thought that my children would be the first in the family to have a traditional Jewish wedding under the huppah, but now Don and I would lead the way.

The Shabbat morning of our wedding, Don and I stepped up to the Torah for our very first aliyah (honor) as a couple. Can you imagine the beauty of this moment? So many times, I had prayed for us to ascend the bimah together (the raised platform from which the Torah is read). It had been fifteen years of simchas without our mutual assent. Donald held my hand and squeezed it as we stood side by side gazing over the Torah. My joy included a flood of memories of "what was not and now is." A dream that I prayed for had come true.

That evening, our home bustled with excitement, clothes, and floral arrangements. Donald and Zachary left the house in their handsome black tuxedos with Tammie and Tiffany in their fancy party dresses. Upon entering the synagogue, we were greeted by more than two hundred guests. Our former neighbor and good friend, Shirley, had designed the ad journal. One of the tasks that Don and I promised to do as honorees was to encourage our friends, family, and business associates to purchase ads. This ad journal raised considerable funds to help the congregation's annual operating expenses. Everyone benefited as our testimonial/wedding supported the synagogue. We laughed and cried over the jokes in the journal and all the well wishes. Evan Dobkins kindly wrote this tribute to us. He beautifully captured our reciprocal relationship with our beloved community:

> Many terrific things are happening this evening, yet as we smile and enjoy ourselves, we also realize that a wonderful chapter of life at Temple Israel will draw to a close all too soon...
> Sandy and Donald have been Shabbat regulars for many years. Long before Donald's conversion to Judaism, Donald sat in our sanctuary learning and participating with the other 'regulars.' Tonight, in addition to this well deserved honor, Sandy and Donald will exchange their wedding vows in a traditional Jewish wedding ceremony, bringing more smiles and perhaps some tears of joy to many of us.
> This evening let us lift our glasses and toast this special couple. We'll enjoy every single moment until the lights grow dim in the wee hours of the morning. Along with all the joy and excitement, we will confront the reality that in just a few months, a new chapter in the life of the Armstrong family will begin. Temple Israel will say farewell to these special people. Chris and I will miss their infectious smiles and warm presence in our lives. Ridgewood's loss will be Hawaii's gain. Life around here will be very different without Sandy

and Donald and I can only imagine how different life on the island of Oahu will be once their new neighbors and friends experience the Armstrong family. One small step for Sandy and Donald, one giant step for the expansion of Jewish life in a far away place in the middle of the Pacific Ocean.

We laughed, looked through the journal pages, drank wine, ate kosher sushi, and relished talking to our friends and family before the formal presentations. After the initial festivities, we were ushered into the main sanctuary for the speeches to begin. Here are the excerpts.

Donald Speaks

"I would like to take a few minutes to answer some questions that you might be having about today's festivities: Why am I remarrying now? Why will Sandy circle me seven times? And why are we moving to Hawaii?

"As many of you know, I recently converted to Judaism. Although we have been practicing Jews for many years, celebrating Shabbat and the festivals, keeping a kosher home and attending synagogue, we have continued to evolve in our Jewish lifestyle. I converted so that I could more fully participate in Jewish life. I can now receive aliyot, read Torah, lead services, and be buried with my wife. At this morning's services, I shared my first aliyah with Sandy as our daughter, Tammie, read from the Torah.

"I didn't realize that I was marrying Sandy on the day of the leprosy parashah in the Torah. Hmmm?!! But in today's Haftarah, we learned how Elisha had advised Naaman to make himself pure by immersing in the River Jordan seven times. After our respective trips to the mikvah, Sandy and I are eager to achieve the special purity of the huppah together.

"I am remarrying Sandy because I want to, and because I am obligated by Jewish law to do so. I also like the idea of making another, more informed, choice. At twenty-three, I really didn't have a clue; but at forty-nine, I will gladly renew my vows.

"I enjoyed teasing Sandy about walking around the groom seven times. She argued that this tradition was too sexist, too conservative, too groom egocentric, and so on. In true rabbinic fashion, Rabbi Gil came up with a number of modern, egalitarian alternatives, which, as is the groom's prerogative, I rejected. But as Sandy and I researched this tradition, we learned that it is imbued with many beautiful meanings.

"The bride circles her husband seven times in order to protect him. Seven is a special, holy number; it symbolizes completion and fulfillment. Creation took seven days, culminating in Shabbat. Now the bride and groom create their own special world, their own palace in time. There are seven days in each week with seven aliyot distributed on the seventh day, Shabbat. The phrase "when a man takes a wife" is mentioned seven times in the Bible. Jacob labored seven years for his bride, Rachel. And just as Joshua circled the walls of Jericho seven times before they came tumbling down, so do the walls between the bride and groom fall as their souls are united. Sandy and I agreed that this tradition would work for us.

"Why are we moving to Hawaii? Why not?!! Many newlyweds make the trip. We plan on staying there for an extended honeymoon. But seriously, what's not to like? The weather is perfect, it's part of the United States, they elected a female, republican, Jewish Governor, and the people are laid back and filled with the aloha spirit. We've already been welcomed into the Jewish communities at Congregation Sof Ma'arav and Temple Emanu-El. Last fall, Tammie and I found a beautiful house on the island of Oahu. It has a fishpond, a mango tree, coconut palms, giant ferns, and a million lizards. So what if it has a few leaks and needs some work; it's only a short walk to one of the most beautiful beaches in the world.

"As some of you know, I lived in Hawaii as a teenager and I always wanted to go back. My father, who is the only retired General that I know who is not a television commentator, and my mother go there regularly. We are also confident that our family and friends will come to visit us often and soon. Some are already scheduled to be there this summer, even before our household goods arrive and the roof is fixed.

"I have eighteen years of memories that are too numerous to enumerate tonight. But since my time is limited, let me get right to the heart of the matter. As a married Jew, I have learned that marriage is like the study of Torah:

"It's often difficult to understand how or why it works, but it does.

"You're not always on the same page as your spouse (but she'll tell you where you should be).

"You hear her commandments, but they're hard to follow.

"Your wisdom and love can only grow with years of hard work.

"Like Torah, my marriage has been and will be a constant source of joy and wonder. As Sandy and I renew our vows, I feel truly blessed. I have the love of family, friends, and community. What king could ask for more? Thank you all for coming tonight to celebrate with us."

Sandy Speaks

"How do you explain fifteen years in just a few minutes? How do you say thank you to friends and family who have meant so much to you for so long? You can't, but maybe throughout these next few minutes I will describe what my life has been like working with Temple Israel.

"The Torah portion I read for Sisterhood Shabbat this past January was from Exodus—

> Then the Lord said to Moses, "Why do you cry out to Me? Tell the Israelites to go forward. And you lift up your rod and hold out your arm over the sea and split it, so that the Israelites may march into the sea on dry ground. (Exodus 14:15-16; Rabbinical 1999)

"Just about then I lost my spot in the Torah and kept going from memory. As my nerves took hold of me, I became acutely aware of people around me. The voice from the bimah of the gabbai resonated, but more than that, I heard voices from the congregation speaking out the words. I heard those words and I heard people guiding me. The congregation 'cried out' as my perfect Torah reading was anticipated. I even heard, 'Just move down a line! You're in the wrong spot!' Then I simply got my footing again and went on.

"This story describes my relationship with Temple Israel. When I drew a blank, should have moved down a line, or was simply in the wrong spot, this community was always there to throw me a word, a gesture, and a direction to follow that would bring me onto a good path—the right path. There were times when I was frightened, when I came to Shabbat services unsure of my place in the world. And somehow, after a few hours of sitting here quietly listening to the service, or meeting a new person who had just walked into our midst, I felt better, more alive than ever. This is what Temple Israel and this community could do for me. After my mom died, the Shiva (the weeklong mourning period after death) set me straight again on my path in life. I had the love and comfort of all of you and I was able to move on and accomplish more and more only because I had your support: to cheer me, to encourage me, to engage me, to cry out to me. I found that Temple Israel and I became engaged in a process, an ever-evolving combination of motion and emotion. You have given us oceans of love tonight, more than any two people should ever hope for in a lifetime. Thank you."

The Ketubah

A very talented artist, Susan Guttman, created our Jewish legal wedding document called a ketubah. The words written in both Hebrew and English are surrounded by pink, blue, lavender, and white flowers that resemble a floral lei. Don and I, in turn, wrote our signatures, "Donald James Armstrong" and "Sandra Marcia Zimmerman," on the document before the wedding ceremony began.

The contract states, "The said Bridegroom made the following declaration to his Bride: 'Be thou my wife according to the law of Moses and Israel. I faithfully promise that I will be a true husband unto thee; I will honor and cherish thee; I will work for thee; I will protect and support thee, and I will provide all that is necessary for thy sustenance, even as it beseemeth a Jewish husband to do. I also take upon myself all such further obligations for thy maintenance as are prescribed by our religious statute.' And the said Bride has plighted her troth unto him, in affection and in sincerity, and has thus taken upon herself the fulfillment of all the duties incumbent upon a Jewish wife. This Covenant of Marriage was duly executed and witnessed this day according to the usage of Israel."

A Walk Down the Aisle

Our daughters were the bridesmaids. They wore flowing lilac gowns with circular floral headpieces draped with ribbons. While in the newly renovated bridal room, Tammie and Tiffany helped me dress in a creamy white, full-length wedding gown decorated with lace and tiny pearls across an empire waist. I wore a short, delicate veil that was a gift from my dearest friend, Amy Rattner. Don and Zachary (our best man) wore matching tailored black tuxedos. I was in a state of pure joy as Don's father, Ed, walked me down the aisle. It was an indescribable experience to walk arm and arm with him. He gave me away to his son who stood handsomely awaiting us. As we approached the huppah, I barely noticed the guests in the pews. All my attention was focused on Donald.

I was getting married again, to a man I had known for a long time, and I had no doubt in our future success. The first time around, I wasn't so sure of myself. We were only twenty-three and had so much ahead of us. Now, twenty-five years later, I knew a lot more about living with Donald. We already had the children—this phase in our lives had been successfully accomplished—and we were entering into a new Hawaiian chapter.

We were leaving so much behind, but hoping to gain even more as newlyweds again. The thrill of adventure was upon us and we were ready to meet the challenge. The wedding ceremony was not only wonderful but also necessary for the future of our new Jewish home. At the same time, we reaped the benefits of the love and support from the entire evening of celebration. Leaving on a high note with this strong support base behind us made us more secure in our decision to move on. The knowledge that we had "done some good in Ridgewood" propelled us into a bright Hawaiian future.

The religious wedding sanctified our relationship. We stood surrounded by our living accomplishments, our children. And now, we had achieved the ultimate, a holy union before God. The wedding ring that I received that day is the one that I wear as a continual reminder of life's potential. We held hands underneath the huppah, a special place for the new bride and groom. It consists of four lovely decorated posts and a cloth draped across the top to make an awning over our heads. It is open on all four sides, like our lives together within a loving community. We were united under the canopy of God's watchful eyes. At the end of the ceremony, Don stomped down on the wine glass. The shattering woke us up out of our dreamy place beneath the secure shelter of the huppah. We kissed and turned to our friends and family awaiting us.

Floral leis were bestowed on the guests as they entered the social hall. Don and I were each lifted up on chairs and danced around on the shoulders of our friends. Everyone was up and clapping, people were whirling, and feet were stomping. The whole room jumped with klezmer music. The merriment went on and on, weaving in and out, circling and spinning. Rabbi Steinlauf and I did the "rabbi spin"—you grasp hands and spin as fast as you can round and round until you almost fall down from being so dizzy. Don, Tammie, Tiffany, Zachary, and I twirled around in the middle of three rings of guests converging back and forth, left and right all dancing the hora. My cousin Lois and I held hands and turned around and around like the "whirligig," our favorite childhood playground ride. The celebration was the culmination of years of friendships and special occasions. My response when asked was purely visceral: "Every piece of me is jumping for joy."

After the initial dancing had calmed down, we awaited the toast. The honor was given to our good friend and Temple Israel's previous rabbi, Rabbi Noam Marans. In his *Jewish Standard* interview (*Turning Point*, 5/2/03 by Joanne Palmer) he commented:

> It's an amazing story. I believe that with the Armstrong's you are witnessing the very rare reality of intermarriage being turned into a Kiddush HaShem—a sanctification of God's name. Decades after they first met, through ongoing study, patience, and community, they arrived together at the conclusion—and specifically Donald concluded independently—that he was ready to convert and thereby unify the family under one religious umbrella...It didn't happen overnight. The conversion was just the completion of an ongoing process in which Donald was living a Jewish life anyway. It was just a question of making that final, very emotional, very critical step. It's the beginning of a new stage and the end of the process of realization. It's in the best interests of a human being who finds himself in this situation, and of his family—and of the Jewish people. The conversion was one of the most rewarding moments of my rabbinate.

The rest of the evening rapidly flew by. Our in-house band, the Maccabeats performed several numbers. And Don, a full-fledged band member, played the electric guitar. We were all on the dance floor begging for encores. Finally exhausted, at two in the morning, we found our car in the parking lot tastefully decorated and written with "Just Married! Be fruitful and multiply. You are an inspiration to all of us!" We removed the cans and ribbons, reminders of one of the greatest evenings of our lives.

We were married among the people we love the most, B'nai Israel, the children of Israel, our family, and community at Temple Israel. For one brief moment, under the huppah, after twenty-five years of life together and fifteen years of Judaism in our home, we were perfected into a union of man, woman, community, and God.

Epilogue

In 2002, Donald and Tammie scouted out neighborhoods on the island of Oahu. They quickly settled on the windward side of the island. They were only going to look, but on the last day of their trip, they found a ranch style house that was within walking distance to the beach and the center of town. Don made an offer on the house and we hoped for the best. Two weeks later, I flew out with Donald and we purchased our new home. It needed a new roof, renovations of the bathrooms, and a covered lanai along the back of the house.

Donald selected the contractor and stayed in Hawaii to work on our new home while I worked with a realtor to sell our house in Ridgewood. The only glitch was that the oil tank failed its inspection and had to be removed. On a frigid winter day, it was finally dug out of our icy front lawn and lifted by a crane high in the air for disposal. It was so cold that the coffee I bought for the workmen had frozen. After three garage sales and one furniture sale throughout the spring, the girls and I waited for school to end so that we could join Donald in Hawaii.

Before we arrived, Donald did very well making friends in the neighborhood. He often invited them over to watch the gecko wars on the backyard window screens. When I finally moved from New Jersey, our new neighbors speculated that I was his second wife and that the teenage children were from his first marriage because I looked too young. I laughed so hard and said, "Oh yes, they're his!"

Our renovated home looked great, but we needed to buy furniture. We all slept on air mattresses and sat on beach chairs for several months. When we called our son in college and told him that we still didn't have beds, he said, "What's wrong with you people?" Our friends Denise and Ben visited us on their way to Australia a month after we moved. Michael, their son, remarked, "Do people in Hawaii sleep in beds?" This was after his air mattress had completely deflated during the night.

The girls and I arrived in Hawaii on July 3, 2003 and early the next morning, we went to the 4th of July parade with our neighbors. We had prime seats on the parade route at the Baxter's home. The annual Baxter Bash featured a homemade gourmet breakfast buffet, free patriotic hats and T-shirts, ice cold drinks, and watermelon. After the parade, we were able to shake hands and take our picture with the governor. What a great way to celebrate our family's first full day in Hawaii. But that's Hawaii for you. The people are so gracious and welcoming.

We quickly settled into our new routines. Donald and the contractor got along so well that Donald decided to go to work for him as a laborer, job runner, estimator, and purchasing agent. He worked five days a week from 7:00 a.m. to 3:00 p.m. After work, he would take a dip in the ocean and then jump in the hot tub. Can you imagine your former Wall Street investment banker jack hammering away in the middle of the street? Or how about him crawling around in restaurant ceilings insulating chill water systems? He even worked inside industrial boilers to repair them. This is a man who rarely picked up a hammer back in New Jersey.

I worked as a substitute teacher in the local elementary schools and when I was certified as a special education teacher, Don stopped working. He spent time doing volunteer work for service organizations like Family Promise (an interfaith organization that provides food and shelter for Hawaii's working homeless families) and FACE (an interfaith organization that pursues social justice issues like affordable housing and health care, immigration reform, and sustainable food and energy production). When Jewish burial space was needed on Oahu, Don developed and now owns a Jewish cemetery called Abraham's Garden.

We became Shabbat regulars at Congregation Sof Ma'arav, the westernmost Conservative congregation. One Shabbat morning I gave the d'var Torah (a word of Torah) and described my childhood surgery. At the Kiddush lunch after services, I was surprised to discover that one of our congregants, Paul, worked on the heart lung machine in South Africa, the same one that was used to save my life. I almost passed out when he described the mechanics of how blood circulated through the machine and my body.

But life in Hawaii for us was not just rainbows, beautiful sunsets, gentle trade winds, and soft sandy beaches. Three weeks into retirement from his construction job, Don went hiking with a neighbor on an expert trail. The ridge hike to the third peak of Olomana was fine. However, at the start of the climb back, the trail rope snapped. Don went over the narrow ridge trail and fell twenty-five feet. A small, strawberry guava tree with a three-inch trunk stopped his fall. Don's shin was miraculously wedged between this little trunk and the cliff face. Fortunately, he never let go of the rope when it snapped. He was able to find a stick, tie it to the end of the rope, and throw it up to his hiking partner. Together they were able to secure and hoist him back up to the ridge trail for the hike home. He suffered nothing more than a bloodied shin and a bruised ego. Don contemplated whether or not to tell me about his close call, since I told him to not go. He said that when he went over the ridge he thought, "I am going to break my back and then Sandy is going to kill me."

We found out later that other hikers have fallen there over the years, and not lived to tell their tales. If the guava tree had not stopped Don, he would have fallen more than six hundred feet. Don said that God was watching out for him and that he must have been saved to do something important. A few weeks later Bernice, the president of Sof Ma'arav, asked Don to be her vice president.

The next year, he was elected president (unopposed) and he continues to lead our congregation to this day (still unopposed).

Another close call came for Don when he had quadruple bypass surgery at Queen's Medical Center in Honolulu. During a routine stress test, it was discovered that he had a major coronary blockage (despite his overall good health and fitness regimen of several hours of tennis four days a week). Our wonderful cardiologist, Dr. Joana Magno, explained that the angiogram showed a major blockage in his left main artery. This condition is colorfully known as the widow-maker.

Before I knew it, the surgeon came into the room to speak to Don and promptly scheduled his open-heart surgery two days later. No time was given for us to worry about this. Don wanted to do this as soon as possible at Queen's Hospital. I could not have made that decision as quickly or with as much conviction.

Three days after the surgery he was released from the hospital. I was astonished that he could be released so soon and I was scared. How would I take care of him? As I drove him home, he sat in the back seat clinging to his heart pillow as fragile as a newborn baby.

The synagogue's annual Hanukkah party at our home was already scheduled for the following week. Don and I decided to celebrate the miracle of his successful open-heart surgery with the miracle of Hanukkah. God had granted us life instead of death. It could have been a shiva minyan instead of a festival celebration. The night of the party, Don received his friends in bed and reminded them to consider purchasing cemetery plots in Abraham's Garden. He laughed and said, "You never know when you might fall off a cliff or be surprised that you need major surgery." He proudly said, "Now, Sandy and I have matching scars."

During my long walks along the beautiful shoreline near our home (the same shoreline shown on the cover of this book), I was inspired to write poetic reflections that appear at the end of the book. Each reflection correlates to a chapter in our lives.

Thank you for listening to me "talk story" about our spiritual journey. I hope that this memoir inspires you to share your own story with your family and friends.

With Aloha,
Sandra M. Z. Armstrong

Bibliography

1. Hertz, J. H. *The Pentateuch and Haftorahs.* London: Soncino Press, 1992.

2. The Rabbinical Assembly. *Etz Hayim: Torah and Commentary.* Philadelphia: Jewish Publication Society, 1999.

Reflections Along Hawaiian Shores

Stepping on Soft Sand

I strolled down the beach today, so self-absorbed that I did not notice the change from soft sand to rocks. I carefully stepped in and out of the silky sand around the rocks, hoping not to stub my toe, until I grew tired of the maneuvering. I realized this was the pattern of my life. I spent much of my time weaving in and out, avoiding sharp, hurtful moments. I wanted my life to be smooth like a walk on comfortable sand. I worked hard to avoid the jagged edges. I began to cry, remembering times when it was hard to step around all my problems.

Eventually, I reached a flat plateau on top of the rocky shore. I stood spellbound as I gazed over the ocean. I sat down on the ledge and soaked my feet in the calm tidal pool below. I was sure that I had reached heaven. The world became a refreshing breeze, as simple as the salt spray caressing my face. I thanked God for my life and prayed for its continuation. I wanted others to share this feeling of infinite beauty and joy. Despite all the rockiness in my life, I yearned to move on. I understood that obstacles made me appreciate the calm, sandy shore.

As I walked back, I managed to stub my toes over and over again. There was no easy way, no well-defined path, around the rocks back to the beach. Pain and mental confusion followed. No clear-cut route caught my eye. It was that soft, sandy path that I longed for, the key to unlocking my fears and frustrations. I passed a couple on the way and warned them to be careful of the rocky path ahead. They asked me if there was a clear passage over to the next beach. I cautioned them by saying, "No, the rocks will take over at a certain point." They gratefully answered, "Thanks, we will take the safer route around." I watched them stroll away, hand in hand, envious that they had taken a simpler route than I did. God wants us to seek Him, to take the smoother path. Then we will walk peacefully on an unencumbered shore.

Prayer is not in Heaven

Our souls are nourished through prayer. It is how we correct and sustain ourselves.

We achieve spiritual growth and success. We contemplate our purpose and yet, we don't understand everything. We can't explain it all, having a limited capacity to reach beyond ourselves. But that doesn't mean we shouldn't try.

Every prayer is a conversation with God. We are given the choice to initiate a relationship that already exists.

We do not live in the days of our ancestors, and yet their prayers were no different from ours. We are one and the same in the continuum of life. God was as real to them as He is to us now. Eternally hearing our collective voices.

And yet, until we decide to pray, God will patiently wait.

Just Being There

Sometimes you can't do enough to help another person in distress—whether it is a family member, friend, neighbor, or stranger. Fretful thoughts intrude. Should I do more? Why do my efforts seem so futile? Will my help be enough?

Stop worrying. All you have to do is be there. We seem compelled to do more because showing up doesn't seem to be good enough. Caught up in the frenzy of doing and redoing, we find it difficult to appreciate the value of just being there. We want to fix problems quickly, hoping they will disappear. But some difficulties take more time to properly resolve, more time than our spontaneous society allows. It is necessary to slow down and ask ourselves, "Is just being there, going to be enough?" Patiently, we realize, maybe "it is."

Each week we attend Congregation Sof Ma'arav in Hawaii, a small synagogue where everyone's participation is important. Sometimes I feel uncomfortable about not participating in the service or sponsoring the luncheon that follows. Eventually, I realize that being there is important, too. Maintaining membership and supporting the service with my family's presence means something. We help by just being there.

As I walked along the beach today, I thought maybe God wants us to be there for Him, too. Caught up in the many details of our lives, we doubt that just being there would have any impact. Could a little time each day spent acknowledging God make a difference? We often forget to express gratitude for all our blessings. It only takes a moment or two to sit with God and just be there.

Radiance

The ocean sparkles with God's love. I saw a million lights shimmer along the water's edge. Could light be alive? The radiance of the ocean mesmerized me.

I glanced down at my feet to be surprised by a large sunspot reflected on the sand. God was the glorious sunspot illuminating my path.

The glistening lights on the ocean reflected my joyous future. As long as I walked toward Him, the future was delightful, dazzling, and full of enormous possibilities.

Abruptly, a cloud blocked the light and the radiance vanished. I continued down the beach knowing this was only temporary. The light would be back and so would His guidance. Regardless of the clouds, I continued moving forward. The ability to keep the faith and stay on course is a human blessing. When clouds roll in, concealing our relationship with God, hope still remains.

Why do clouds block our way? We don't know, but we wait patiently. A few minutes later, the clouds rolled past and pure light shone on my path.

And then, I made a mistake. I turned and walked in the opposite direction down the beach. The brilliance of the sun trailed behind me. My path was now uncertain. An inescapable loneliness prevailed. God was nowhere to be found. And my life was not the same.

As I continued to walk the wrong way, I felt the warmth of God's rays embracing from behind, gently urging me to turn around. So I did.

What Stops Me?

The ocean is placid like a piece of glass—calm, cool, and inviting. I am walking in the hot sand following in the footsteps of a person who I do not wish to follow, yet I keep going anyway. Is this my path in life? I walk on the dry sand, miserably trudging along. I am trailing behind someone else, knowing all along that it is not right for me.

I see the glistening ocean water inviting me to jump in and find relief. I am stubborn and resist. I walk along the water's edge feeling the gentle water soothing my tired feet. Still, I refuse to jump in. I am neither here nor there, just in limbo between the water and the shore, walking alone. I am parched, fretful, and hot. My mind wanders and it's hard for me to concentrate. I am not ignorant of the relief that the water will bring me, as I look over to see others splashing around. But, I hold back and resist the plunge.

What stops me from jumping in? I can blame my parents for not raising me right. I can blame my past. I can blame my husband or children for the demands they place on me. Or I could blame myself. I desire it, and then I stop myself, hoping that walking in the hot sand, along the shoreline will be enough—when it is not.

I spot a dry, withered vine clinging hopelessly to the sand. I pulled it up. It had no blossoms. It was barely attached to the earth. "Look, I have left behind this shriveled root to represent my time on earth. I wish I had spent more time with God, my faith, and a belief in eternity. If only I had jumped into the cool waters of salvation earlier, I would not be leaving behind this rotten, ill-defined root, as proof of my life and existence."

I waited until the very end of my life to jump into the comfort of the water. I looked back and said; "Why was I so stubborn all those years, when the serenity of the water and the peacefulness of the sea was all I ever wanted? Why did I waste a lifetime before experiencing God and this piece of heaven?

I slid ever so quietly into the calm water. I floated and relaxed like never before. I will go on like this forever and forever. As I float and look at the clouds above, I realize that I can no longer speak. I can no longer hear; my ears are covered with water and only muffled sounds get through. I am in a different world now.

The opportunities to tell my children and grandchildren about the bliss I have found are lost. I missed my chance to describe the comfort of lying in God's arms and the importance of spending one's life in the soothing waters of His creation. I saw it, resisted it, and then experienced it at the end of my life. I was stubborn. I chose to walk along the sand, to spend my days in limbo along the water's edge. I never jumped in until it was too late.

We are Living Works of Art

As I walked to the beach today, it occurred to me that so much of life appeared to be perfect like the Plumeria flower that I discovered lying on the ground. It was an exquisite, faultless creation. I thought how different is this blossom from a human? It has no will or ability to choose between right and wrong. Yet it is one of God's glorious masterpieces, a delight to all.

What about us? We are living, breathing works of divine art. We can reach great heights both intellectually and spiritually. We are formed to sanctify life and add holiness to the world.

On the way back from the beach, I found another similar blossom, as beautiful as the first, except that it had wilted and lost its vibrant color. Yet its powerful fragrance remained.

Do people leave earth in the same manner? Do they die releasing an essence that permeates our lives? Do family and friends continue to say Kaddish—the mourner's prayer—honoring their presence on earth?

As they turn to dust, will they be remembered?

Mother May I?

Small baby steps, giant leaps, or sometimes the right twirl places you on the proper path. If this sounds familiar, it's the game we played as children called Mother May I? The goal is to tag the leader who is calling out the steps. First one to the caller wins.

Now we are adults and asking God, "How many steps forward shall I take toward You, and what kind of steps shall I take?" Moving toward religious observance does not have to be boring. It can be an enjoyable adventure, like child's play. Yet it is the best game of all. As you weave your way through the opportunities to help others, your life gets better.

Does God have a sense of humor? We do, so why shouldn't She? And are we not made in Her image? When you trip and fall on the way to the leader, pick yourself up and laugh it off. God will laugh too, and lend you a hand.

Worship is dynamic, exciting, and fun. The universe is filled with human potential. Goals can be achieved through baby steps, giant leaps, and sometimes just the right twirls.

Complacency

On the path to the beach today, I trudged through rugged, deep sand. My heart pumped harder to find another direction. Eventually, I came upon a clear paved pathway in the park along the edge of the sand. It was a relief to be walking on smooth ground again. I gazed up at the swaying treetops shielding me from the heat of the day. The gentle breeze brushed against my legs, inviting and encouraging me. How much is life like this?

At some point, we will reach a new peaceful plateau. Previous effort on the right path will lead us there. It is then that we need to remember who we are. Life, when it is good, is to be continually appreciated and enjoyed, not ignored due to complacency.

Walking farther along, I discovered an elderly person on my path. Do I pass her, or simply watch as she meanders down to the water's edge? I am patient. I wait for her. She turns one way and I turn another. Do we remember to wait for other people as their paths cross ours? Do we understand that others are as valuable as we are, no matter how young or old?

Every year at Yom Kippur, Jewish people go to synagogue to begin collective repentance—please forgive me as those who I have wronged have forgiven me. We look at how we, as individuals, can strive to live a better, holier existence. We remind ourselves to think of God throughout the year. When we move along easily, instead of trudging deep in the sand, we need to stop, pray, and say, "Thank you, I am grateful to you. I acknowledge your presence in my life." We remember to use every available sense given to us to experience God.

And never take our lives for granted or give into complacency.

A Dip in the Ocean

We come into the world immersed in the water of our mother's womb.
We go out of this world dry as dust of the earth.
Water renews us, invigorates us, sustains us, and maintains us.
We are composed of water. Our bodies crave it.
We cannot exist without it, yet water exists without us.
We cannot exist without God, yet God exists without us.
Water is beyond us, bigger than us, part of us. Like God.
We enter the mikvah and say a prayer, looking for renewed strength.
We depend on Her direction. We depend on Her love.
When we immerse in the water, we dip back into the waters of life.
We are provided for again. Water encircles us, enfolds us, and embraces us.
We depend on the water to purify our souls,
To create a mother's love for Her child.

A Perfect Union

I couldn't get out of bed today. It was one of those days when I would rather stay curled up into a ball and let life pass me by. I made myself get up for my walk to the beach. But, the lethargic feeling stayed and I couldn't shake it off. Could it be low blood sugar? Could it be a feeling of being overwhelmed and not facing up to my responsibilities?

I made it to the beach. As I walked along the water's edge, I was startled by my shadow walking in front of me. My thoughts drifted as I focused on her. We strolled along the beach together. I had questions for her. Is she insecure? Is she lazy? Does she waste time on details that don't matter? Does she have trouble concentrating and paying bills? Does she resist and put aside important responsibilities? Is she patient with her children? Does she nag? Does she repeat herself a million times at home to make herself heard? Is she looking at the world with enormous possibilities? Does she have the ability to change? My shadow walked ahead confidently. She never felt alone because God was always with her, and a part of her. My shadow was everything I wanted to be and more. The perfection I desired.

Suddenly, she disappeared. What should I do now? I wanted to follow her. I needed her patience, strength, and stamina. She was everything I wanted to be, but could not always be. She was gone and I missed her.

As I turned around and walked back down the beach, I spotted my shadow, behind me. My potential was back. The ocean sparkled with the light of possibility. The future was again bright and limitless. This time around, I led the way. I was the powerful one, the positive influence. I could accomplish everything. I had faith that God would see me through the tough times, my moments of insecurity, and those days when staying in bed seemed to feel a whole lot better than getting up.

www.ingramcontent.com/pod-product-compliance
Lightning Source LLC
Chambersburg PA
CBHW071713040426
42446CB00011B/2050